Partners in (

Gaynor Tilby

Text copyright Gaynor Tilby © 2023 All rights reserved

Dedication

This is my story. A story of growing up deaf in a hearing world. Deafness is a lonely disability, an invisible one which many thousands of people will attest to.

In telling my story I share the challenges of being deaf which many hearing people find difficult to comprehend. My book is of hope and joy. Largely in part to being matched with Indigo in 2012. An amazing and beautiful hearing dog from the charity, Hearing dogs for deaf people. He has brought lightness and visibility to my disability for the first time in my life.

My work in the Criminal Justice System is a rewarding career and I pay tribute to the hard-working colleagues wherever you are. I have had the privilege of working alongside some of the most dedicated and kind people since 2006. They continue to contribute to making our communities a safer place to be. I have sought out permission for those mentioned in this book. I thank you. I believe it gives my book flavour and essence. It gives insight for the reader, of the impact that Indigo has had on many different people, working in a challenging role.

This book would not have been possible without the support and love from the hundreds of volunteers who give their time freely to Hearing Dogs charity. Volunteers work alongside the trainers to socialise, and train puppies to be the next generation of skilled hearing dogs. The Charity receive no Government funding. The amazing fundraisers support the cost of training these skilled dogs. Many, many other volunteers work behind the scenes to make the charity what it is today. You are all paw-some! Thank you.

A mention to my beautiful friends, Lesley, Denise, Janice, Cat and Barbara who were willing to read my first draft and give me encouragement. Giving me constructive feedback has enabled my book to make sense!

Lastly and by no means least, my soul-mate, Ralph. Without you, this book would never have seen the light of day. You patiently read my very first rough pre-draft and your suggestions were invaluable. Your ongoing support and love you give me on a daily basis inspired me to write my story. With all my love, always.

In buying this book, you dear reader, have contributed to Hearing Dogs for Deaf People. All royalties of this book will go to the charity. I thank you from the bottom of my heart.

Contents

HMP Haverigg, here we come! 7
Isolation 9
Chinese Whispers 12
School of life 14
Career Choices 17
Hairdressing Apprenticeship 18
Holidaying in Wales? 21
Challenging My Disability 22
Living With a Deaf Person 25
One Memorable Day and New Horizons 27
My Application for a Hearing Dog 30
Meet and Greet 33
Learning the ropes with Indigo 35
New Staff Member 39
Let Sleeping Dogs Lie 42
Establishing A Work Routine 44
A Shocking Doorbell 46
Partner In Crime 47
Love Hurts 49
Cone-headed Indigo and a new routine 52
Assessment Time 54
Drugs in a Pocket? 57
Weekend Lie-ins 59
Easing The Tension 60
Bed And Breakfast Volunteers 62

Highway Walks 64

Dartmoor Prison 65

Hospital Fan Club 68

Volunteer Speaker 71

The Notorious Smell 74

Toilet Dramas 77

Working Away From Home 79

Pampered Pooch 82

Brownies and Demonstration Dog 84

The Missing Hot-Cross Bun 87

Celebrity Ambassador 89

Chocolate Labrador 93

A New Chapter Awaits 95

Canoeing the Lakes 97

Crufts Here We Come 99

Reality Check 103

Indigo Weaves his Magic 104

Virtual Talks 106

Retirement Beckons 109

The Challenge of Great Gable 111

New Kid on the Block 113

Big Paws to Fill 116

Photos 118

HMP Haverigg, here we come!

I stood in front of imposing steel gates which loomed large above me. The sign helpfully informed those approaching the gate that its height was just over fifteen metres. I looked up at the coiled barbed wire entwined in circles, sat atop the fences either side of the gates which was in stark contrast to the sign also saying, 'Welcome to HMP Haverigg.' The year was 2019, and it was my first day of work as a probation officer at Her Majesty's Prison, Haverigg. Standing at the entrance triggered a sense of foreboding, and I was sure my thumping heart would be heard by anyone who happened to be near me. With a mixture of trepidation and excitement, I made my way to the gatehouse.

I had previously been working as a probation officer in the community for the past thirteen years, supervising men who had been released from prison. Now I was about to embark on working with those who were still serving their sentences behind bars. I felt some nervousness starting my new job with a new team and a range of questions were spinning around in my head. Would I be able to hear and understand my new colleagues and the men I would be working with? Would there be lots of background noise in the office? Would there be enough space for my assistance hearing dog, Indigo to settle by my side whilst I worked?

As I mused on these thoughts, I took a deep breath and looked down at Indigo, my assistance hearing dog, and my 'ears' for the past eight years. 'What do you think buddy? Can we do this?' He looked up at me with his soft brown eyes as if to say, 'You've got this, Mum.' We had been through so much together in our eight years of partnership and I knew that whilst he was by my side, we could confidently tackle any new challenges that came our way, together.

Walking up to the reception area, I was met by a stern looking, burly prison officer stood behind a glass office window. I informed him of my name, adding that it was my first day reporting to work at the prison. He asked for my ID: 'See this list of banned items?' he said, pointing to a poster on the wall. 'Have you brought any of these with you into the prison?' I studied the poster carefully, going through a mental checklist in my mind. Mobile phone – I had left mine firmly at home that morning. Metal cutlery – I had not brought any kind of cutlery, as I had assumed my new workplace would have some; maybe the healthy salad I had packed for lunch was not such a good idea after all! 'No, I have none of those things on me.' I assured him. His stern expression remained unchanged as he made a phone call to my new line manager, Sean, and handed me back my ID. I stepped back from the window whilst I waited for Sean to arrive and escort me through the prison and unlock the numerous gates dividing the many areas between reception and my new desk.

Suddenly the burly prison officer beckoned me with his finger, to return to the window. Slight panic grew within me about the banned items, and in that moment, I again mentally checked I had nothing on me that was not allowed. Nervously I walked up to the glass panel and leant forward to strain to hear whatever my fate was going to be. On the other side of the glass, the prison officer also leaned forward and slid his hand in the hatch beneath the window. I looked down and there in the hatch was a dog biscuit for Indigo. Any tension I had, melted away. Indigo looked up. Sensing there was some food for him he peered at me expectantly, waiting for his biscuit. I burst out laughing and, in that moment, I knew we were ready to meet our new challenge.

Whilst laughing at this moment of acceptance from a colleague with Indigo by my side, I reflected on my own journey in becoming a probation officer. Growing up as a deaf person in a hearing world had brought many trials and tribulations. I understood that all those experiences had helped shaped the person I was to become.

Isolation

I grew up in the seventies in Amersham, Buckinghamshire, a town in the southeast of England, along with my parents and an older brother. My earliest recollection of something not being quite right with my hearing was being given grommets. This involves an operation under anaesthetic whereby a small ventilation tube is inserted into the eardrum to allow air into the middle ear and prevent a build-up of fluid. Unfortunately, the first attempt to insert these was unsuccessful and so I had two further operations, but to no avail.

My mother was adamant in her theory that the grommets had damaged my hearing although she offered no evidence as to why she thought this was the case. None of my family had hearing problems. I realise now it was probably difficult for my parents to reconcile with the fact that their longed-for daughter had a disability. To this day I still do not know what caused my deafness.

Specialists in the ear, nose, and throat department at our local hospital, suggested that fitting me with two behind-the-ear hearing aids, would support my development to learn speech and enable me to follow conversations. This was an era where disabilities were not so openly talked about, and there was a distinct lack of support and awareness. I am sure that is why my parents did not want me to be any different from the other children growing up around me.

When I was very young, before going to sleep at night, my hearing aids would come out and Dad would hold my bedside clock to my ear. 'Listen Gaynor,' he would say. 'Keep listening to the clock.' And gradually he would move it further and further away. He believed he was 'training' my ears to hear better and by doing this he thought he could magic my deafness away. My parents' attitude about my deafness to others was that 'Gaynor is not deaf, just a bit hard of hearing.' It was an attitude which in retrospect helped me to be able to achieve what I wanted, but it also left me with a legacy in later life that deafness was something of an embarrassment and should be hidden away.

My earliest memory of being deaf within a hearing world, was at nursery school. It was the era when nursery schools supplied all the children with a mini bottle of milk and a biscuit at break time. To create some order, the teacher would call each child up by name, to pick up their treats at the front of the class. I can still recall the feelings of unease sitting at the back of the classroom, straining my neck, and doing my best to see the teachers face and watching out for the shape of her soundless mouth saying each child's name. Loving my food as I do, I was anxious not to miss my turn to pick up my mini milk bottle with its customary straw inserted in the top, along with my biscuit. Thankfully I do not recollect ever having missed out, but it was how I learnt the art of being alert with my eyes in order to understand everything I would need to hear in the future.

It was time for me to start school and my parents were given the option of either sending me to a specialist school for deaf children, or to a mainstream school with some speech therapy and extra support for a couple of hours each week. Their belief that I was only 'a bit hard of hearing' meant that they believed mainstream school was the best option for me. As a result, I was the only deaf child in the school and learnt to quickly adapt with my hearing friends. It was a time when there was little technology to support a deaf person other than with my hearing aids. There was also little awareness of diversity, and I was simply expected to fit in with my hearing compatriots.

A strong early memory from junior school was when I was around the age of six and it was play time. At the edge of the playground, there was access to an outdoor swimming pool via a gate. The pool was part of the school and regularly used for scheduled swimming lessons and galas. It was fenced off and as a natural water baby, I loved peering through the fence to watch the other children enjoying their swimming in the clear blue water. During one particular break time, a swimming lesson was taking place and I became totally mesmerised watching the children through the fence, splashing in the pool.

Unaware that the whistle had blown, signalling it was the end of break time. I had continued my enjoyment of watching the children swim. When I eventually turned round, expecting to see the playground full of children, I found that I was completely alone. No-one had thought to tap me on the shoulder to tell me that the whistle had gone and it was time to go back to our classroom. My six-year-old self was upset and embarrassed that I had not known it was the end of our breaktime. I can remember creeping quietly into the classroom hoping that no-one would notice that I was the last child coming back from the break. At the same time, trying to hold back hot tears of distress.

Chinese Whispers

Speech therapy sessions were a vivid memory for me. During my junior and middle school years, I was taken out of the classroom for an hour or so each week, to work with a variety of different kind and caring ladies who, it seemed to me, had chosen their careers wisely. The range of sounds I struggled with most were the higher pitched ones. My bespoke practice speech book, which I carried around with me was a book of nursery rhymes. 'Repeat after me,' the speech therapist would say 'Incy-Wincy spider, climbing up the spout,' and 'She sells seashells on the seashore.' I often smile at these rhymes now, thinking about the challenge of saying them clearly when you have had a couple of glasses of wine let alone with a speech impediment! Not that, alcohol was something I consumed as a child growing up, I hasten to add! I think the speech therapy must have paid off because later in life, many people have since remarked that I have excellent speech and that they had not realised I am deaf.

Growing up, I developed a way of fitting in and not drawing attention to myself if I had not heard. I was also very good at deflecting the need to hear, and one of the ways I did this was to play the class clown or chat to friends which negated hearing. Although I see myself as a natural chatterbox, I was keen not to appear unfriendly or aloof because I had not heard, and so I would often chat away or play act in order to make friends. As a result, most of my end of year class reports were: 'Gaynor can be a bit silly,' and: 'Gaynor talks too much in class.' I think if the teachers had delved a bit deeper into the reasons for my silliness and endless chatter, they might have understood that I was just a child trying to fit in and make friends, and that it was all a cover to hide my deafness.

I loved doing all the activities my childhood friends enjoyed and was enthusiastic to join the Brownies and Girl Guides. I found the challenge of earning badges fun and would eagerly scour the badges book to check what activities I would need to participate in to earn a particular badge. I treasured the leaders for both Brownies and Girl Guides and felt that they made the weekly meetings both interesting and fun-filled. However, there were occasions when the activities they organised required being able to hear.

One of these games was called Chinese Whispers. The game would start with the leaders whispering a sentence to the person sitting next to them in a circle. That person would then have to whisper what they had heard to the person sat next to them. By the time it got to me I would fix my fake smile that I had become so proficient at, and make up whatever sentence came into my head and whisper it to the girl sat next to me! There was much hilarity on the finished sentence not being remotely similar to the one that started the game! I had become so good at not drawing attention to myself, that no-one seemed to make the connection that playing this game with a deaf child meant that there was little or no chance of a successful round, as I simply could not hear what was being whispered! If anyone had looked a bit more closely, they would have seen past my false smile to notice my eyes welling up, smarting with humiliation as I cringed with red hot embarrassment.

School of life

My next move was to an all-girls secondary modern school in Amersham. Computers and technology were still in their infancy and so dictation and listening were an important part of the curriculum. I found that if I sat at the front of the class, I could follow most of what was being said. However, if a particular teacher liked wandering around the room, I had to crane my neck to see their lips for lipreading. My other methodology to try and follow was to sit next to school friends that had good handwriting. Whilst we were dictated lessons to write, I would look over at my friend's book so I could copy what they had written. It always upset me if a particular friend decided that they were not going to let me do this for one reason or another and covered up their book so I could not copy.

It was no surprise that the subjects I did well in, tended to be with the teachers that had the clearest mouth and facial patterns for me to lipread them. I look back on this and my adult self, realises that a simple solution to this would have been for them to give me the book or a photocopy of the script that was being read aloud, although; I think the teachers felt that we would remember it better if we had written it down for ourselves.

Another example of the importance of being able to see the teachers' mouth patterns in order to lip read them was in school assembly. We would tumble into the great big main hall to hear the head-teacher speak to us all. I would crane my neck to try and see her from the middle of the hall. There were no microphones and if I was not sitting at the front, I could not use my lipreading skills to understand what was being said. I would sit in my silent world, admiring the latest hair styles or fashionable shoes of the girls who were sitting near me. It passed the time of assembly and I would follow the cues of the others if they laughed or clapped, not knowing what message had been imparted to the school that day. Now and again, if I thought I had missed something important from the speech, I would pull a close friend aside afterwards and ask what had been said.

Sadly, during my school days there were several girls who seemed to delight in bullying me because of my deafness. Taunts such as 'Deaf-aid' and 'Turn your hearing aids up' were a constant reminder of being different, and that made parts of my school life a misery. I did my best to ignore them and continue with my learning but now and again their taunts really affected me. Like the time I was walking in the school grounds during a lunch break, enjoying the fresh air. I spotted one of the ring leaders loitering on the path I was on. My heart sank as I approached her, she started voicing her opinion of me and my deafness. As I got closer, my heart beating faster by the second, I could see she was about to kick me. Reacting quickly; I grabbed her raised leg. Instinctively, to stop herself falling backwards she grabbed hold of my coat.

It must have looked a comical sight with her hopping on one foot not going anywhere. She screamed at me to let go of her leg, and I calmly told her that once she had let go of my coat, I would release her leg. She realised I was serious in my intent and duly let go of my coat. I released her leg and breathed a sigh of relief, as I watched her scuttle away looking very embarrassed in front of her gang of friends. Thankfully, she left me alone after this very unpleasant incident.

Another vivid recollection of bullying in secondary school happened during a lesson when we were required to read to ourselves. We all had our heads down reading our books when I noticed that one of the girls in the group was passing a note round for everyone to read except me. What I found out later was that the note told all the class to start mouthing what they were saying without any voice so that I would think my hearing aids had broken. Noticing the room was very quiet, I looked up from my book and saw all the girls just moving their lips without any sound. When one of them mouthed 'Are your hearing aids broken?' I knew that they had conspired to make me the butt of their jokes. Laughing it off I told them 'No my hearing aids are not broken as I can hear myself.'

These were stark reminders that I was different. I just wanted to be accepted as an equal and enjoy my schooling like everyone else. Sadly, this just made me more determined than ever to cover up my disability and not draw attention to myself.

Career Choices

It was time for me to make a decision about what I would do for a career after leaving school. I felt frustrated with both my careers advisor and the formidable Miss H, a hearing consultant who was involved in my regular hearing check-ups at the local hospital.

My enduring memory of Miss H was being somewhat frightened of her. I would enter her room at the hospital and there she would be sitting behind her intimidating big desk, wearing a disk-shaped head mirror on a band around her head. I imagined she was a space alien, not being able to fully see her facial expressions or make full eye contact. I now know that head mirrors are used by otolaryngologists in the examinations of the ear and throat. When she used it, she would swing the head mirror down to look through the hole in the middle with one eye. She would then position a light source so that it shone on the mirror's parabolic surface, and move her head to reflect the light rays to examine my ears. I much prefer today that the doctors shine a penlight into my ears to examine then than the head mirror contraption that Miss H used. A penlight is so much less intimidating.

After the obligatory ear examinations, Miss H would cross examine me about my career ideas. Every job I suggested was met with a disdainful comment telling me that there were too many barriers for me to cross as a deaf person. Even as a professional she was focusing on my disability rather than emphasising my abilities. I decided that I wanted to become a hairdresser. I had a desire to work with people. My love of talking and genuine interest and curiosity about other people were skills I knew would stand me in good stead. When Miss H asked me how I would manage to take bookings on the phone if I could not hear. I promptly informed her that I only intended to work in salons that employed receptionists!

Hairdressing Apprenticeship

I was lucky enough to gain a place at Harrow College on a full-time two-year placement learning hairdressing, wig-making, and make-up. Mr Bowmer, the motivating and inspiring course director, had instilled in me the belief that despite my disability, I would be able to learn the craft. The lecturers working with Mr Bowmer included a Mr Laholt and between the two of them they gave me the inspiration, passion, and the skills to become a competent hairdresser. My fellow cohorts were a wonderful warm bunch of fellow students with a mixture of ethnic backgrounds, ages, and diversity.

It was a big turning point in my life as a deaf person. For the first time in my life, I was not made to feel embarrassed or different, but simply accepted for my abilities and who I was. The only occasion I was reminded of my deafness was a day when our cohort was to travel into central London to participate with a well-known hair company. As we gathered in the classroom ahead of our trip, my fellow students and Mr Laholt asked me if my hearing aids were whistling as there was a high-pitched whistle emanating within the room. I can usually hear if my aids are whistling and confirmed that it was not coming from me.

We set off on the train for London. However, I was informed that the whistling was still following us. I decided to conduct an experiment by turning off my hearing aids completely and I asked my fellow students if they could still hear the whistling which they confirmed they could. I felt somewhat exasperated at this point. I could not continue the day with my hearing aids switched off, but equally, I knew this whistling was starting to annoy everyone. I searched in my bag to see if there was anything on me that could be causing it and to my surprise, I discovered a spare hearing aid I had forgotten about. It had a battery in it and, by chance, switched itself on, hence all the whistling. I pulled the offending item out of the bag and took out the battery and declared the culprit. Lo and behold the whistling ceased and we all had a giggle about it.

The day went without further incident, and I thoroughly enjoyed going to London and seeing round the company and listening to how they came up with ideas for their products. The next day, I arrived promptly for our classroom session led by Mr Laholt. I sheepishly admitted that it was my spare hearing aid that had caused all the noise the previous day. Imagine my embarrassment when he said 'You do realise we had called up the building engineers yesterday to try and establish the cause of the whistling.' Thankfully, he had a good sense of humour, and could see the funny side to the whole scenario.

I made the most of every opportunity offered to me at the college and worked hard. I found I had a natural flair working with hair and challenged myself to learn all I could. I also found ways of communicating with clients with the trick of looking in the mirror to lipread what they were saying. I felt a strong sense of responsibility not to let the college down when they had invested so much in training me and given me the chance to prove that I was so much more than my hearing impairment.

After two years, I graduated with flying colours. I had found my vocation. I was happy. Some months later I was invited back to the college to watch the students' annual hair competitions something I had enjoyed in my student days and having been a proud winner the previous year. That night, as the competition was coming to a close, Mr Bowmer stood up to make a speech. He announced that a major hair company had donated a special trophy to the college. He went on to say that after some deliberations, the staff had decided that they would award the trophy to an outstanding student, who 'despite overcoming much adversity, had excelled as a student and had gone on to be an exceptional hairdresser.' I was speechless when Mr Bowmer said 'Gaynor, come and receive this trophy!'

To this day, I still have the trophy and it is an important reminder to me that when someone opens the door of self-belief, and possibilities, whatever barriers I may face as a deaf person, I would have the courage to go forward and overcome them. It was a far cry from the negative voices of the doomsayers at school who had told me so many careers were not an option because of my deafness.

Holidaying in Wales?

I did many jobs as a hairdresser but vividly remember my first job after graduating working for Rina in her salon. Still doing my best to hide my deafness I became an expert at nodding and smiling at the customers I could not hear or lipread when making conversation whilst cutting their hair. On one occasion a young man with a strong Welsh accent came into the salon. After checking exactly what kind of style he wanted, I proceeded to cut his hair. I struggled to understand him as he chatted away to me. As a coping mechanism, I politely responded with a nod here and there, and a 'Yes, yes!' in what I hoped were the appropriate places. He paid his bill and off he went very happy.

Later that afternoon, his mother came into the salon and asked me if I was coming to Wales with them at Christmas? I was somewhat astonished and asked her why she would think this. She replied, 'My son seems to think you are.' I was totally unaware that the friendly young Welsh man was happily asking me to join him and his family on a trip to Wales at Christmas! I am sure with my affirmative responses and smiles; he could not believe his luck when I agreed to join them having just met me! Rina, the salon owner had been listening to this exchange and with much laughter cautioned me: 'Gaynor, don't pretend you have heard when you are cutting a customer's hair.' It was a valuable lesson to me, and also a glaring reminder that it was not something I could continue to do as it certainly could end up placing me in more tricky situations that I would have to squirm my way out of!

Challenging My Disability

During this time, I met my husband, Ralph, through my brother. Ours was a relationship that started out as a warm and supportive friendship. I have always maintained I married my best friend and soul mate. We are a great team and Ralph was, and continues to be, a huge support to me in so many ways, but in particular around my deafness. He was instrumental in reinforcing to me that deafness was not my fault and was certainly nothing that I needed to keep apologising for, sadly the word 'sorry' had become my mantra.

One year, I discovered that, Ralph had secretly installed a hearing loop in our lounge to help me hear the television clearer. A hearing loop works by streaming the sound from the TV directly into hearing aids. I still chuckle at how he did this as a secret Christmas present for me. That Christmas morning, Ralph switched on the TV and turned the volume down citing that he needed to keep an eye on the weather. We started to open our Christmas presents and Ralph said: 'The phone has just rung and there is someone who needs to speak to you.' I automatically switched my hearing aids onto the loop setting and suddenly I could hear lots of different sounds that I knew were not coming from the phone. I looked around confused, only to see Ralph smiling at me and mouthing the words 'Look at the TV.' It dawned on me that the sounds coming through my hearing aids were of the weather forecast. My eyes welled with tears. I knew that Ralph's actions were not only from a place of love but also to remove barriers of communication for me.

I had become used to not hearing things and, in many ways, had thought it was part and parcel of my silent world. Ralph was far more investigative of what aids may be out there to support me. Computers were starting to be mainstream, and he was keen to install a home computer. In the early days of computers, Microsoft Encarta, a digital multimedia encyclopaedia published by Microsoft, was launched, and I can remember the first time Ralph clicked on it to show me. I was blown away at the visuals of it and felt somewhat elated that finally a visual world was opening up to me, it was in such a sharp contrast to my silent world. I realised how much I had missed at school and wondered what a difference it would have made if technology had been available when I was growing up.

Ralph was able to see, at first hand, the daily struggles I had being deaf. When I set up as a mobile hairdresser, he could see how I was struggling to hear the addresses of potential customers who I would be visiting for their first appointment. One particularly painful conversation happened as I was doing my best to hear the address of a new client. I had not explained at the start of the conversation that I was deaf and, when it came to finding out where she lived, she gave me a house name. I asked for a house number but as she lived in a village, all the houses just had names. I struggled to hear what she was saying and guessed the name began with a high-pitched letter as I was only able to hear the second part of the name 'Garland.'

I could fell the panic rising in me as I struggled to hear her. Unfortunately, when I panic, I struggle even more to hear. I found myself close to tears. I started to stammer out my usual apology that I was deaf and could not hear her. I finally asked her to speak to my husband to tell him the name of her house which was Treegarland. I simply could not hear the soft sound of the 'T' which along with phonetically pronounced 'p,' 'm' and 's' make up the higher pitched range of letters of the alphabet. Putting the phone down, I burst into tears and, as usual, Ralph patiently waited for my sobs to subside.

He gently told me that I needed to stop apologising for being deaf and as it was not something I could do anything about. He reminded me that I needed to share with people that I was deaf in the first instance. I brimmed with tears and started to sob, releasing all the hurt I had felt during my school days when I did not want to bring attention to myself as a deaf person. My deafness had made me feel as though being unable to hear was my fault. I had convinced myself that I could carry on in this way. Ralph reminded me that adults tend not to be as cruel about disabilities in the way that children are, but in order to help and support me people needed about my deafness in the first place.

Ralph had summed up something that I had not been able to articulate until now. It was a powerful conversation that continues to remain with me on a daily basis. I came to a kind of acceptance of my own limitations and the different dialogue I needed to adopt for my future self. It was a turning point in my life to realise I am not invincible. We started to look at what solutions were available for deafness. One very useful device we had installed was a telephone with an extra earpiece. This enabled me to talk to the potential client whilst Ralph listened and wrote down the most important parts of the address.

Living With a Deaf Person

I often think Ralph's patience and understanding knows no bounds when I do not hear sounds, but I think even his patience was challenged one time when I accidentally locked him out of our house. We were living in Buckinghamshire at the time and just had a new front door fitted, but I was not aware that when the key is left in the lock on the inside, the person on the outside cannot not get their door key in. One morning, Ralph had a meeting scheduled in another part of the country and was required to set off early. After waving him off in my dressing gown, I put the key in the door and went upstairs to have a shower and wash my hair. I had taken my hearing aids out and in doing so, was unable to hear anything at all. Once dried and changed I popped my hearing aids back in and could hear some clattering outside the open bedroom window. Looking out, I could see Ralph arranging a ladder against the open window. I called down to ask him what he was doing and in a somewhat exasperated tone, he shouted up 'Let me in!' He had forgotten his wallet and could not get in as I had left the key in the lock on the other side and there was no response from me when he rang the doorbell. Fortunately, he had a garage key and so, using his initiative, he fetched the ladder out of the garage so that he could climb in through the open window. I think he was somewhat relieved to see me peering down at him, out of the window before he started wobbling up the ladder as heights do not make him feel entirely comfortable. It was another example of the impact of not being able to hear every day sounds such as doorbells or alerts. Luckily Ralph made his meeting in time.

I went on to do many different roles as a hairdresser, including working on a roadshow for a well-known hair company. This involved travelling around the country demonstrating the company's products. Wherever I was staying, to ensure I arrived in time for work, I had a portable alarm clock that would vibrate under my pillow. It always worked but was an unpleasantly harsh vibration under my head. On one occasion, I arrived home late on a Saturday night after travelling home from working in the

North of England. I hastily threw my overnight bag in the wooden wardrobe to unpack the next morning, sleep being uppermost in my mind. The next morning, unbeknown to me, I had forgotten to turn off the waking time on my vibrating alarm. Ralph told me it took him ages to work out what the strange noise was. In his semi-conscious state, he said it sounded like Martians had landed! He even looked out of the window to check for UFOs! Our wooden wardrobe was acting like a sound box, reverberating my alarm clock in the loudest way possible. Thankfully, he realised what the offending noise was and quickly rummaged in my bag to turn it off. Any idea of a lie-in that morning was not realised for poor Ralph.

One Memorable Day and New Horizons

I continued to progress in my career and worked in a variety of settings, including working in a popular health spa and teaching hairdressing. Eventually, I decided to set up my own mobile hairdressing business with an emphasis on weddings. This involved offering a whole package of creating elegant bridal styles and make-up for the bride's special day. During this time, I also decided to set myself a challenge and run the London Marathon. Not being a natural runner, I knew this was going to be hugely challenging.

I had decided to apply for a charity place and knew that my chosen charity would be Hearing Dogs for Deaf People. I had read and heard so much about the amazing work the Charity did in training dogs to support deaf people and was in awe of how the dogs could change a deaf persons' life. I was lucky enough to secure a charity place and the months of hard training and pounding the streets began. I followed my training plan to the letter and in April 2005 I was one of the many proud runners approaching Buckingham Palace and then seeing the finish line on the horizon.

I crossed the line wearing a spotty T-shirt and a hat with long ears to represent a dog. I now knew that anything I wanted to achieve was possible with enough determination, will and hard work. I was very proud to go to the Charity's headquarters in Buckinghamshire to meet with someone who had a hearing dog and hear first-hand the difference her dog had made to her life. I felt very emotional meeting someone who, like me, understood the frustrations, isolation, and loneliness that deafness can bring. It was a magical moment being able to hand over a cheque for three thousand pounds to the Charity from the sponsorship money I had raised with my running efforts.

After the marathon, I realised that there was a big part of me that was still unfulfilled in my career, so I started looking for a new challenge. I had spent many years working as a hairdresser, and still had a desire to make a bigger difference in people's lives but did not know how I would go about this. I had this nagging feeling that there was another career out there that would challenge me a bit more and enable me to develop a different skill set.

I had always wanted to study at a higher level and technology to support deaf people was getting better and better all the time. The legacy of being told in my school days that I could not do a particular job because of my deafness was slowly being removed. During this time, Ralph was working in London as a management consultant for the Metropolitan Police and I was able to stay with him every few weeks. I met the team of police women and men who Ralph was working with and was struck by their commitment to making their communities a safe place in which to live. Not only this, I was inspired by the way in which they were diligent in their roles and their ability to maintain a sense of humour despite the challenges of their job.

Soon after I achieved my medal in the London Marathon, and following many meetings with Ralph's colleagues in the Metropolitan Police, a job advert in the local paper jumped out at me and piqued my interest. The advert wanted trainee probation officers with transferable skills, and I was intrigued enough to want to know more. After an open day listening to trainee probation officers and identifying the skill set required to do the job, I was determined to give it my best shot.

Following a lengthy application process, I was offered the job and was astonished to find out on the first day of my new job that I had been successful out of 1,600 applicants. Knowing that there were only 65 jobs available in the south west, I was fully aware that I had been offered an amazing opportunity. I felt that they had looked beyond my disability and that I had been judged on the skills that I could bring to the role. It was an exciting time and, as someone who was approaching their forties, an amazing chance to have a second career. The training was spread over two years and I worked hard. I felt the same way that I had felt years ago in my hairdressing training. I did not want to let down my employers who had invested so much in training me. It was to be another opportunity to demonstrate that I was so much more than my hearing impairment.

I graduated in 2008 with a B.A. Honours in Community Justice Studies and an NVQ Level 4 in Community Justice - Work with Offending Behaviour. It was exciting that at the end of our studies all the students in the south west were invited to a celebration day to mark the end of our training. I enjoyed meeting the other graduates within the area and sharing our experiences. That afternoon, after lunch and speeches, an announcement was made about an award. The Linda Sage Memorial Award, in memory of a staunch supporter of probation practice, would be presented to the trainee who had submitted the best NVQ unit regarding probation practice. I could not have been more surprised when my name was announced as runner up in the whole of the south west division. I was riding on a high for some time after this incredible nomination.

My Application for a Hearing Dog

After my graduation I worked in the North Devon team. I moved through the various teams and settled on working for a small team managing men convicted mostly of domestic violence and sex offences. I had been working as a probation officer for three years and my job involved supervising a case load of men who had been sentenced to both community and custodial sentences. The job involved meeting many different people on a day-to-day basis, going to prisons, courts and attending multi-agency meetings in order to manage the risks that the service users posed. In addition, I was working with the programmes team delivering interventions for men convicted of domestic violence.

It was around this time that I decided that applying for a hearing dog would be of enormous support for me. The days were exhausting exacerbated by the effort of having to listen carefully to many new voices. In addition, every time I met new people, I had to explain about my deafness so that they would face me directly and speak clearly. I was beginning to feel that my working environment would be enhanced by having an assistance hearing dog as well as keeping me safe when working in different environments; for example, if fire alarms should go off. The other important aspect of my decision to apply for a hearing dog, was for the dog to alert me to the sounds around our home that I could not hear.

The application process for a hearing dog is not quick and that is as it should be to ensure the right match is found for each partnership. In the first instance, I needed to send audiograms, a doctor's note to support my application and also a note of support from my work stating that they could see no issues with me having a hearing dog in my workplace. In addition, I received both a work and home visit to check out my environment. Part of the assessment also involved meeting an ambassador dog with their partner at my home.

I eagerly awaited Boots, who has a very special role at the Charity. He spends time with those who have applied for a hearing dog, so that they can see what having their own dog would be like. I enjoyed meeting Boots and his partner from Hearing Dogs and hearing about how Boots fits into his partners' everyday life. In particular, the importance of routine and ensuring that the welfare of your dog is paramount. I was also to take Boots shopping with me with the partner giving me tips on how to make sure that Boots stayed safe with a trolley and other people walking near me. As I took Boots' harness, I felt petrified that I might be holding the lead too tightly or that the trolley would bash over his paws and hurt him. I need not have worried because he was definitely a professional when it came to negotiating supermarket trolleys.

I waited for the Charity to find a suitable match for me. I knew that my lifestyle was one which was going to be quite bespoke due to the numerous locations I worked in such as courts, prisons, and various offices - all of which could be a challenge for a dog that was not confident. I also enjoyed a weekly run and visualised a dog running alongside me at weekends to keep fit. I knew that I would need to be patient in being found a suitable match.

At the time of my application, Hearing Dogs for Deaf People was undergoing huge changes. Founded at Crufts in 1982, the Charity would use dogs needing a home from dog shelters and train them to be hearing dogs. However, the Charity was struggling to find enough suitable dogs, with the right qualities to train as assistance dogs. They realised they needed to be smart with the Charity's money and so at the time of my application, they had changed their business model to start a small breeding scheme to meet the increasing demand for trained dogs.

Breeds such as Spaniels, Labradors, Miniature Poodles and Cockerpoos (cocker spaniel crossed with a poodle), were the breeds that responded well to the training. It meant that I waited a bit longer than normal and five years passed since my initial application. The Charity kept me updated and informed of what was happening and so each letter I received was met with quiet anticipation that a match would soon be found.

Meet and Greet

In 2012 I received the exciting news that Hearing Dogs for Deaf People had a match for me. The dog was named Indigo and the trainer felt that he would be perfect for my needs and lifestyle. A photo was enclosed of a beautiful black Labrador Retriever cross, and I chuckled to see his eyes peering back at the camera clearly saying: 'Love me.' I was informed that Indigo was at the charity's Beatrice Wright training Centre in Beilby, East Yorkshire. The Charity has two training centres, the other one being in Princes Risborough, Buckinghamshire.

Living in Devon, the irony was not lost on us that the centre furthest away was the one where Indigo had been trained. As luck would have it, my mother-in-law, Jean, had moved 20 years previously to Filey in Yorkshire, which was an hour's drive from Bielby training Centre. My own parents had died when I was in my early 20s and Jean and I had developed a close bond over the years. She was a mother of two boys, and she always made me feel that I was the daughter she had wished she had. Jean was over the moon for me that I was matched with a hearing dog. She had previously been the owner of a Golden Retriever herself, a breed that she had loved and enjoyed for a decade, so could not have been more delighted for me that Indigo was a Labrador Retriever cross. Jean's proximity to the training centre enabled us to stagger our journey by staying with her first and then driving to meet Indigo for the weekend.

Ralph and I spent a moving weekend in the Beatrice Wright Centre, referred to inhouse as the BWC. It was here we met the trainer, Nicky, and Indigo for the first time. Nicky wanted to see us first to explain Indigo's cheeky nature, and his love of food. Her face became grave when she told us about his naughty traits such as stealing socks, pulling them off your feet and running away with them. She searched our faces to ensure that we were comfortable with this, and we nodded that it was something we felt we could cope with. Whilst she went off to fetch him, I looked at Ralph and we both burst out laughing about the character we were about to meet. We both have a natural sense of fun and felt that Indigo was going to be a good match for me. When Indigo was brought to us to meet him for the first time, it was love at first sight and I could not wait to get to know my new 'ears.' We stayed for the weekend, taking him for walks and chatting to Nicky about his many character traits.

The centre has individual houses on the site where new partnerships can get to know their dogs. On waking the next morning, Indigo jumped on the bed and gleefully licked our faces. It was as if he was telling us he was very happy to have met his new partner. After spending a weekend with Indigo, it was time for us to tear ourselves away and drive back to Devon. I was to return in a few weeks' time and spend a full week at the centre to learn how to work with Indigo.

Learning the ropes with Indigo

Spending a week with Indigo at the BWC was both tiring and enlightening. Although Indigo had already been trained to alert me to all the different sounds around the house, I now needed to learn how to respond to him so we could develop our bond of working together. In addition, it is a huge responsibility having a dog in tow when walking in shops, cafes and using public transport, as generally the public does not naturally expect a dog to be under a table or walking beside a trolley in a supermarket. I spent a week doing different activities every day and going to different environments to learn how to work with Indigo and ensure his safety.

The Centre is really well designed and has a number of buildings kitted out like mini houses. Here, they can practice all the sounds that the dogs are trained to alert a deaf person to. The houses simulate the future home that a hearing dog will live in. And this enables the dogs to acclimatise to the sights and sounds of a home. They are kitted out to mimic the sounds they will come across when they move in with their deaf partner. Sounds such as the doorbell, cooker timer, alarm clock, telephone, smoke alarm, fire bell and, if a deaf person lives with someone else, being able to get their attention when they are in a different room. This last sound is known as 'the call.'

I had a thoroughly enjoyable week, learning to work with Indigo and making sure I understood when to reward him with food treats and when not to. Indigo had been trained to alert me to different sounds by nudging me with his nose on my leg. Once he had done this, my job was to tell him he was a good boy, immediately deliver a treat and ask him 'What is it?' This was his cue to take me to the source of the sound and, as his reward, he would get another food treat.

Being a Labrador Retriever who loves his food this was clearly a great game for him. We entered the mini house, and he instinctively knew what he was there to do because he started to nudge Nicky with his nose before any sounds had even started. She did warn me that he was too clever by half and had a sense of expectation of extra food. I chuckled to myself thinking he is certainly not daft for wanting his extra treats.

To start the process of working together I was handed a squeaker. Indigo had learnt to associate the squeak with nudging his nose on the leg of the person emitting the noise. Indigo gave me a firm nose nudge on my leg when I pressed the squeaker and I gazed into those beautiful brown eyes looking up at me seeming so keen to get this right. It was an emotional moment of connection; I was beginning to place my trust in this being who would now be taking on the role of being my ears.

Nicky then set off the range of sounds and Indigo responded on cue with firm nose nudges. When the doorbell rang, he nudged me and after receiving his treat and being told he was a good boy, I asked the question 'What is it?' Off he went to the door encouraging me to follow him. The cooker time was set using a mobile timer placed on a table. Nicky explained to me that Indigo was not to go to an actual cooker as this was likely to be a hot place and dangerous for him. On cue, Indigo gave me a nudge when the timer went off and patiently took me to where we had placed it on the table.

We then tried out the alarm clock in the upstairs of the house. My job was to pretend to lie in the bed asleep whilst the alarm clock was set up. Two minutes lying in the bed pretending to be asleep and waiting for the alarm to go off felt a very long time. On cue when the alarm sounded, Indigo used his front paws to jump half on the bed letting me know that I was to get up. It was a far cry from the harsh vibrating alarm clock that I had been used to under my pillow.

We then practiced 'the call.' This involved Nicky being in a different part of the house and calling Indigo. Once he had been rewarded by Nicky, she gave a command of: 'Call Gaynor,' Indigo keenly ran to fetch me, nudging me with his nose first and then taking me to Nicky. Little did I know at that time, this was going to be such an important alert some years later when Ralph needed my attention. The telephone was the next task to conquer. Although I cannot hear on the phone, it is an important sound as it includes an answerphone I can play back later to Ralph if necessary.

The final sound that Indigo had to learn was the smoke alarm. Being a danger signal, this required Indigo to respond in a different way to all the other sounds. After nudging me, instead of going to the source of the sound, Indigo would lie down on the floor. This alert is a clear signal to tell me that I need to be alert for danger and take appropriate action. I was in awe of the work the Charity had put into training Indigo to alert me to all these sounds I had never been able to hear. It was at that moment that I thought how incredibly lucky I was to have my application accepted to receive this amazing hearing dog.

Later that week during my training, it was time for my first outing with Nicky and Indigo to a nearby town centre to learn the ropes of having an assistance dog in tow. As we entered a café for a cup of tea and cake, I realised my life would never be the same as Nicky explained that it was my role to pick a safe place to sit so that staff would not trip over Indigo. I earnestly scanned the café for a safe place for us to sit and realised that in future I would need to think ahead when planning trips to cafés and restaurants to ensure the safety of Indigo, and if I was going to be able to relax. I picked out a table near a wall which had space to put Indigo alongside. I was relieved that Nicky informed me that the table was a good choice, and we made our way over to sit and enjoy tea and cake.

I was pleased to see Indigo settle at my feet with no expectations that there would be food for him whilst we were eating. We finished our tea, and Nicky informed me that if I needed to use the toilet before we left that I would need to take Indigo with me. Having found the toilets, I discovered to my horror that they were all single cubicles. I realised that negotiating 36kg of Labrador Retriever and myself into a tiny cubicle was going to be a challenge.

I placed myself into the cubicle and looked at Indigo to follow, he warily eyed the space that I was trying to encourage him into. He decided he would have none of it and firmly sat outside the cubicle, not budging. Slight panic grew within me as I tried to coax him into the tiny space. I was wondering what to do and whilst musing over this dilemma, relief washed over me when I saw that the slightly bigger cubicle next to me had become vacant. A gentle pull on his lead and Indigo finally came in with me. Whilst he was clearly not impressed that he was cooped up in this small space and with little room to move around, he nevertheless stood patiently whilst I sat on the toilet. I breathed a sigh of relief that I had overcome this hurdle. As I sat down on the pedestal, I remembered that I had to give Indigo praise for getting it right. I gave him a number of affirmative praises, speaking clearly saying 'Good boy, good boy'.

Walking back into the café I noticed a couple of ladies I had passed going into the toilet giving me rather strange looks. I sat down with Nicky and relayed my challenge of the single cubicle and it suddenly occurred to me how strange it must have sounded hearing someone saying repeatedly that they were a good boy in a female toilet. Nicky and I burst out laughing! Those ladies must have wondered what on earth was going on behind that cubicle door!

New Staff Member

It was time to take Indigo home after completing my week at the training Centre. Nicky bade me farewell and gave me strict instructions to ensure that the first weekend remained calm and quiet for Indigo so that he could settle into his new home. After a long drive from York to Devon, we were glad to get home. The weather in May was its usual unpredictable self. Lashing rain and a howling wind at sixty miles an hour had brought down the power line at the front of our house and it was waving precariously above the drive. Ralph told me that it had involved a panicked call to Western Power Distribution and he was awaiting their arrival.

I walked through the front door with Indigo feeling excitement and caution. As part of my application, having a canine partner who would get on with our two cats was stated as being extremely important to me. The training centre had a resident cat, and Indigo had been completely chilled out in its company. My caution on entering our home was in part because Indigo had not yet encountered our pint-sized peril named Sooty, who was a tiny black cat with serious attitude. On entering the hall, Sooty declared his presence by placing himself at height, three steps up our stairs, puffing himself out and hissing at the same time. He was certainly not going to take any nonsense from this new black stranger who had the audacity to enter his home. Indigo took one look at him and sensibly decided to give Sooty a wide berth. Our other cat, Rocky sprang as fast as he could out of the house and took himself off onto the roof of the shed, where he wailed pitifully that his home had been invaded and his peace disrupted. This was not the calm and quiet household I had envisaged for a first weekend together!

After settling Indigo in for the weekend, my new Partnership Instructor, Lyndsey came to our home the following Monday in order to help us practise the sounds that Indigo had learnt back at the centre, within his new home. In addition, she would be there to support me whilst I introduced Indigo within my work environment. Partnership instructors are employed staff that support all the hearing dogs and their deaf recipients for the lifetime of the dogs. This unique working relationship enables the deaf person to build confidence with their new hearing dog partner, and any issues that may arise can be worked on with the support of the instructor. Their role is an important one as they ensure first and foremost the wellbeing of the dog; in addition to being a fount of knowledge in canine behaviour.

Lyndsey arrived in the morning and after a meet and greet from Indigo, all-important coffee and cakes were devoured before we began the business of introducing Indigo to the sounds, he learnt at the training centre. The centre had provided me with a squeaker and this was the first step of reinforcing the sounds that Indigo was familiar with. A firm nose nudge on my leg assured me that Indigo had remembered his training and was ready to have the sounds around the house set off to practice.

Receiving lots of lovely extra treats, the Labrador Retriever in him was very keen to show me where the sounds were. After a lovely morning working with Indigo and then a break for lunch, we ventured into town to practice wheeling a trolley in my local supermarket. I felt immense pride walking with Indigo by my side. It was hard to ignore other customers' faces when they spotted Indigo and smiled at seeing him hard at work. A few people wanted to chat to me about how he worked and naturally wanted to make a fuss of him. I was pleased when they asked if it was OK to stroke him and I thanked them for asking me first. I realised then that future shopping trips were never going to be the same again and I would need to factor in extra time for meeting and greeting whilst doing my shopping.

The following day, Lyndsey returned to the house, and we agreed that, as I had booked a week off from work, that it would be a good opportunity to introduce Indigo to my office colleagues. Entering reception, Jackie our receptionist could not stop cooing over Indigo and telling him he was a gorgeous boy. She informed me that the team were in a team meeting and suggested that as it was the regular weekly meeting for our office, it was an ideal opportunity to go in and introduce Indigo with everyone in the same room together. I tentatively took Indigo along the corridor to the group room and peered through the window to see everyone sitting there. One of my colleagues saw me and excitedly beckoned me in as all my team colleagues knew I would be bringing Indigo in to meet them.

During the previous few weeks before travelling up to the training centre, I had been talking nonstop to anyone who was patient enough to listen about my new match. It was time to introduce everyone to Indigo. Walking into the group room, one of my colleagues, Wendy told me to walk Indigo round the table to say hello to everyone and so that is what I did. There were exclamations all round about how beautiful he was and how smart he looked in his Hearing Dogs uniform.

Indigo behaved impeccably in a completely non-plussed way, taking all the attention in his stride, and clearly loving the extra strokes and cuddles he was receiving. After making sure I had introduced everyone it was time to show Indigo his bed which was already placed in my office. Walking into my office and settling Indigo on his bed next to my desk, he looked so contented, and it felt that the final piece of my jigsaw had slotted into place. I burst into tears of happiness.

Lyndsey spent the best part of a week supporting me. We visited all the local places I was planning on taking Indigo so it did not feel so daunting for either of us. It was time to say farewell although she assured me that I could email her or text her if I had any problems. She promised she would come and visit me again in a few weeks' time to ensure all was going well. My working week was to begin with a new set of paws joining the team.

Let Sleeping Dogs Lie

Part of my role involved spending one day a week as a member of the court probation team. This was to prepare pre-sentence and oral reports at the local magistrates' courts to support them in passing the appropriate sentences. There was an allocated seat for probation in the court room alongside the prosecution outlining the case before the magistrates.

The court setting is a very formal affair with everyone present rising when the magistrates enter or leave. The lead magistrate, known as the Presiding Justice or chair, is formally addressed in court as "Sir" or "Madam". I usually found court duty a stressful part of my job, often struggling to hear everything that the prosecution and the defence solicitors were saying when outlining their arguments to the magistrates. My main concern when addressing them was whether I had heard them correctly. I would place my portable hearing loop in the middle of the court room to help pick up all the sounds however, if someone did not have clear lip patterns, I still struggled to hear everything.

It was slightly daunting taking Indigo into the court for the first time hoping that he would be comfortable enough to settle down next to me. I need not have worried. I had rolled out a soft bed for him and he had lain down on it almost immediately when the court proceedings started. Relieved in the knowledge that Indigo was comfortably settled, I was able to concentrate on listening to the prosecution outline the various crimes that had been committed. These ranged from offences such as drink driving and, assaults, to repeat shoplifting. The next hour or so was uneventful from a probation officer's viewpoint and I was not called on to write any reports that morning.

In the session, various duty solicitors earnestly represented their client's cases to the magistrates. They suggested community-based agencies to support their clients as a viable and non-punitive pathway which would mean that they did not end up with a Probation and Criminal Justice led sentence. I was earnestly listening to the options presented to the courts and as I did so, a loud, deep, and slow snoring emanated from the bed beside me. I looked down to see that Indigo was in mid dream state. I sneaked a glance at the magistrates and I could see that they were doing their best to ignore the snoring and remain impassive. However, I observed that one of the magistrates was doing his best to keep a straight face.

I was relieved when the morning session came to a close and thankful that Indigo had not gone into full noisy dream mode which would have probably involved yelping in addition to his deep snoring. The clerk asked everyone in the court to rise as the magistrates were taking a break for lunch. As I stood, I gently tapped Indigo on the head and, quickly rising from his slumber, he was on full alert. He immediately sat upright on his back legs as if he understood the formality the occasion required of him. Finally with only court staff in the room, the magistrates burst out laughing as they could see this hearing dog was also following court etiquette.

Establishing A Work Routine

Indigo fitted easily into my day-to-day routine and was quickly adopted by all my colleagues in the office team. Probation work is never the same each day or predictable. However, what was predictable was the routine that Indigo managed to create for himself when going into my office in the morning. After entering the office via the back door there was no way that I could rush past the courts team as he insisted that we had to say good morning to them all.

A cheery hello and fuss for Indigo was always the norm from my colleagues before they would say hello to me and catch up with what they were expecting for the day ahead. Before I could check in at reception, I had to walk down a corridor passing the office of the wonderful and caring victim liaison officer, Jo. Her role was a difficult and challenging one and involved working to empower victims of crime and contribute to community safety by providing relevant information about probation supervised sentences. In addition, her role was crucial in ensuring the victims' views and concerns were conveyed to the prison or parole board when release from prison was considered. Information she had was invaluable for us as probation officers and supported us in the decisions we made regarding protecting the public.

Jo's role was a tough one. Indigo realised she had a soft spot for him and would resolutely stand outside her door until it was opened, and he could do his meet and greet and receive his morning cuddle. It was as if his cuddles had become an accrued canine right of employment in the office. Jo was soft on Indigo and would often sit on the floor with him and give him a huge hug and cuddle. As this was taking place, I would have a quick catch up with her and find out if she had any new information that I needed to be aware of when writing my reports and managing my cases. After having his fuss from Jo, we would finally reach reception where he would demand yet another fuss from the lovely receptionist, Jackie, who had quickly fallen in love and adored him. Only after he had received all the required cuddles from staff was I finally able to make my first coffee, log onto my computer and start my day!

A Shocking Doorbell

Indigo arrived in May when the weather was glorious. My mother-in-law, Jean, who loved animals, delighted in hearing my regular updates on his progress. Ralph was working away from home for a week in June. The day he was due home, Indigo nudged me to let me know that someone was at the door. I opened it and my stomach lurched when I saw a policewoman standing there. She asked me to confirm my name and then informed me of the shocking news that Jean had died by taking her own life.

A painful time followed where, as well as coming to terms with the loss of a much-loved parent we had to try and make sense of the unanswered questions surrounding her suicide. Being in Devon and having to sort out her home in Filey, North Yorkshire also added to the stress.

Nature has always had a soothing effect on me. The daily routine of walking Indigo before work where I watched him enjoying sniffing and trotting along by my side enabled me to have some calming head space and grounding before the demands of my time in the office. Blue skies, bright days, and walks at the weekends together with Ralph were an important time to talk and think about the days and weeks ahead.

Partner In Crime

Part of my role as a probation officer in the community involved overseeing men and women who had been given community sentences by the courts and make sure that they successfully completed their sentences. This involved regular meetings with them and putting in place interventions to support their rehabilitation so that they could go on to lead law abiding lives.

I found that getting to know the person's life story was an important part of working with them as it enabled me to understand them better and adapt how I worked. An important part of a probation officer's training is to work with the information that the person shares with you, and the behaviours that you see in the room. Whilst it is important that targets are met, it was also important that service users felt listened to and were prepared to share their experiences and perceptions. Without condoning the behaviour that had led to their convictions, building a rapport and trust enables me to find ways to engage with the service user and motivate them to change the behaviour. I knew from my own experience that if someone gives you a chance, believes in you and listens to your story, you have a better chance of succeeding in your positive goals.

I had this in my mind when listening to *Gary*, one of the men I was working with who had been convicted of serious domestic violence on his then girlfriend. His own history of growing up in an abusive household was all too familiar with other men I had listened to. However, *Gary's* story was a sad tale of growing up with a father who genuinely had not listened to him or believed in him. He sat in my office, telling me of the occasion when someone had set fire to him. Suffering third degree burns, an ambulance was called and, at the same time, his father turned up blaming him for having set fire to himself.

Gary told me about the hurt he felt and the feelings of rejection. At that critical point in his life as a burns' victim, all he wanted was affirmation of love from his father and to be told everything would be alright. During this conversation, Indigo was lying in his bed settled next to me. The tears rolled down *Gary's* cheeks and, just at that moment, Indigo stood up, walked over to *Gary,* and rested his head on his lap as if to say: 'It's OK.' I reflected to *Gary* that both Indigo and I were seeing the pain of that day for him and Indigo was letting him know that it was important to talk about how he felt.

I felt at that moment, that Indigo had captured the mood beautifully, and it is to *Gary's* credit that he recognised that he needed some formal counselling to come to terms with his father's violence and attitude towards him. I often think of *Gary* and wonder if Indigo's presence had been instrumental in that moment, giving Gary the courage to sit through his distress while being comforted by a warm black canine's head on his lap, giving him unconditional love, something he had been craving from his father all along.

Love Hurts

The role of a probation officer is rewarding, and no two days are the same. Constantly evaluating and reviewing the risk of men and women who have committed offences, does mean the job is a full on one. I had watched Indigo happily munching the long grass during his walks, and thought nothing of it until some weeks later when Indigo showed signs of being very poorly indeed. One evening Indigo refused his food and wanted to sit on the cool grass in the garden. Not wanting me near him, he kept getting up and moving away from me any time I stepped closer to him. Becoming more and more concerned, I called Ralph to observe his behaviour with me.

Indigo started shivering and instinctively I knew something was very wrong. He was definitely not his normal self, and I enlisted Ralph to phone the vets and relay what they said, back to me. We drove him to the emergency veterinary practice and were met by a warm and kind vet who checked Indigo over and declared his shivering as a sign that he was not feeling well. Perplexed as to why he might be reacting like this, the vet assured me that they would find out what was wrong, but they needed to keep him in overnight for observation and would x-ray him the following morning to see what the problem was.

Leaving Indigo at the vets was heart-wrenching. I lay on the floor with him, tears spilling down my cheeks. It was remarkable to think that I had only been with him for two months, but in that time, he had turned my life upside down in such a positive way. The raw emotions from the loss of my mother-in-law in such an unexpected and heartbreaking way made Indigo's precarious hold on life seem so heightened. Through the sobs, Ralph and I explained to the vets we had only just lost his mum. I did not want to lose this beautiful boy so early into our partnership, we had too many other adventures to enjoy before his time was up.

After a sleepless night worrying about Indigo, the vets phoned Ralph and told him that they would need to carry out emergency surgery as the x-ray had shown copious amounts of grass stuck in his stomach. I had not been aware that Indigo's munching of long blades of grass had created a problem for him and that he could not digest the grass or get rid of it through natural waste. The vets informed Ralph that the operation was touch and go and that there was only a 40% chance that he would pull through as it was such a major operation. They told us this in order for us to prepare ourselves for the worst but assured us they would do everything they could to save Indigo.

I emailed my partnership instructor at Hearing Dogs and poured my heart out to her. I blamed myself for not knowing that Indigo should not have been eating long grass. I was genuinely frightened that I would appear to be a negligent recipient for allowing Indigo to become so ill and that he would be taken away from me. The Charity quite rightly keeps the rights of ownership with Hearing Dogs. This means that if a dog is mistreated, the dog can be removed as the welfare of the dog is paramount and plays an essential part of the Charity's mission.

The vet was a wonderful communicator and kept us informed of what was going on. After the operation, he phoned to tell us that in his career, he had never seen anything like it in a dog's intestine. The grass had entwined so tightly it was like a thick coil of rope. No wonder Indigo could not retch it or toilet it out, it was just too thick for his body to cope with. My partner in crime had certainly been through a serious operation.

Despite the odds being stacked against him, the operation, which had taken four hours, was a success. The vets had taken amazing care to ensure that Indigo was well looked after. Some days later, when it was time to pick him up, the receptionist told us that they had taken him out of his pen so that he could quietly sit by their sides while they worked. Indigo had spun his magic on them, and they had all fallen in love with his gentle charisma.

When the vets brought him through, wearing a cone of shame around his neck to stop him licking his wound, I burst into tears. Seeing him for the first time since his operation, I felt the raw emotion of potentially losing this beautiful being, who had started to be my invaluable partner in crime at work. It was a magical moment when we took him home after his ordeal with strict instructions for him to rest and recuperate. There was to be no sound work practice and only short gentle walks in the garden and locally, also we did not want Indigo trotting about in the garden and eating anymore long grass.

In preparation for his home-coming, our back lawn was trimmed to within an inch of its life, and has remained that way ever since. That evening, with Indigo lying down by my side with his head on my lap, the opening ceremony of the London Olympics 2012 was televised from the London Stadium. I felt a huge surge of pride for our country hosting this magnificent opening and I am sure so many of the people in this country felt the same way. I watched with tears rolling down my cheeks, in awe of the incredible choreography that Danny Boyle had created for the nation. I pondered that I too, had a little Olympic hero sat beside me who had come through so much.

Cone-headed Indigo and a new routine

Indigo grew stronger and stronger by the day. However, I am sure like most dogs, the unfortunately nicknamed 'cone of shame' is a frustrating piece of apparatus for any dog to wear. Not being able to lick his wound or move around normally was frustrating for him. As he became stronger, he took out his frustration with the cone by knocking the back of our legs with it. I am sure it was a deliberate act as the nudge of the cone appeared to be quite firm rather than accidental to the extent that Ralph started calling him 'Cone-head the Barbarian!'

Happily, it was not too long before his wound healed, and we were able to remove the cone from him. Shortly after all of this happened, my lovely partnership instructor from Hearing Dogs came to see me. She assured me that there was nothing I had done wrong, and that Indigo had shown no previous signs of eating grass being a problem for him. As she stood in our back garden, she admired the beautifully shorn lawn, meticulously cut so that there would be no repeat experience of grass munching.

It was an emotional moment taking Indigo back into the office as I had been going to work without him. Many of my colleagues would ask for a daily update on his progress and when I brought him in for the first time since the operation, I could tell by their reactions that I was not the only one who had been missing him. There was plenty of fuss for Indigo, and he quickly settled back into his morning routine of going round to each colleague in their different rooms to receive the compulsory good morning cuddle and scratch behind the ears.

It was with pleasure, that I noted Indigo had started to form a lovely bond with Jackie, our receptionist on the team. Jackie took no nonsense from any of the service users and should any of them be rude or abrupt she quickly put her stern mother's voice on to bring them back in line. It usually worked and she was held in high regard by them. They would often be seen having a chat with her whilst waiting for their individual key worker or probation officer to fetch them from reception.

Indigo had sensed that Jackie adored him and it was becoming very mutual as he loved to visit her in the reception area whenever he got a chance to do so. At the end of the working day, Jackie would come to our upstairs office and inform us she was going round the building to check that all the windows and doors were secured. Not long after Indigo had returned from his sick leave, he showed an increasing interest in joining Jackie on her end of day routine. I suggested that she might want him to join her going round the building whilst I finished off typing my notes for the day.

I am not sure who was the more delighted, but Indigo happily trotted off with Jackie to accompany her in her role as caretaker for the office. About twenty minutes later; the very happy duo came back to my office with Jackie proudly stating that Indigo did not leave her side as she went round the building. She told me that colleagues were delighted to see both her and Indigo fulfil the important role of closing windows and securing the building. Needless to say, this was to be another routine that Indigo developed for himself in our probation office.

Assessment Time

A few months passed. Indigo and I had established a working routine of walks in the morning before going into the office, and then the important lunch time walk to break up the day. Indigo settled beautifully whilst attending meetings and when it was time to do our weekly shop he behaved impeccably, sitting to attention whilst I browsed the shelves. He continued to excel at his sound work, enjoying the practice of us setting off the sounds before going to work and at the end of the day.

Being a Labrador Retriever, the promise of treats for getting his sound work right, turned it all into an exciting game. He was always looking for the next opportunity for having fun and food! The Charity ensures that all Hearing Dogs work to a required standard, are of good health enjoy their walks and have time to play. To this end, they assess all newly placed hearing dogs a few months into their partnerships by sending an assessor to observe the dog's behaviour and sign them off as a fully-fledged hearing dog partnership.

The day arrived when I was to be assessed with Indigo and an assessor from the Charity travelled all the way from Wales to meet us. She was friendly but clearly had a job to do and held her clipboard resolutely to her chest in order to tick off how Indigo responded to the sounds around the house. I was slightly nervous as it was important that Indigo showed off his skills and demonstrated that he was worthy of the full rights granted to a registered hearing dog. Thankfully, he clearly enjoyed his sound work, nudging me confidently when we set off all the sounds. After this demonstration, it was time for him to be observed whilst out walking, both on and off lead. I decided that I would take the assessor on our usual work day morning walk. Indigo knew the route so well and I knew he would have an opportunity to be on and off lead to show the assessor that he checked in with me regularly. This is an important part of a hearing dogs' behaviour, as the dog needs to keep alert to their partner and in order to respond immediately when they whistle or call. This is essential should they need to be recalled quickly for any reason.

Indigo walked calmly beside me on his lead for the first part of our walk as we were on a country road. Further into the walk, we reached a safe path, deeper in the beautiful Devon Countryside. I took off his lead and he happily trotted off, sniffing around, and exploring the verges and hedgerows as I chatted to the assessor. I was pleased to see he was checking in regularly with me whilst we were chatting and thought to myself how well it was all going.

We turned round to walk back to the house and just as I caught myself thinking we had it all in the bag, Indigo decided he had other ideas! He shot off down the path and no amount of calling or whistling him was going to get him back. He was clearly a dog on a mission, and I could feel myself getting hotter and hotter as the feeling of anxiousness grew.

I quickened my step and could hear his deep bark further along the path. When I caught up with him, he was standing at an open-slatted wooden fence watching, and barking at a small Dartmoor pony. Fortunately, the pony seemed completely indifferent to Indigo's noisy attention as it carried on grazing. I hastily put his lead back on and turned to the assessor as I blustered: 'Indigo has never behaved like this before.' I spent the remainder of the walk explaining to the assessor it was not the usual behaviour I had encountered from Indigo previously and how surprised I was by him running off. My mind was furiously working overtime, and I fretted that Indigo was not going to pass his assessment.

When we arrived back at the house, I was still hot and flustered and dreading the outcome of the assessment. Luckily, we still had the shops for Indigo to show how well behaved he could be. I was relieved when he demonstrated a beautiful sit and settle as I browsed in the aisle of our local shops with the assessor looking on with her tightly clasped clipboard. I am sure Indigo was on best behaviour at this point knowing that he had pushed the boundaries earlier. At last, the day was coming to an end, and I anxiously waited to receive the verdict on whether Indigo had passed his assessment.

My sheer joy and relief were probably palpable when she told me that he had passed. I could have hugged her. She then gave me some sound advice about calling him back immediately if I observed him getting over excited to prevent him running off again. She also imparted some very sound advice which has remained with me to this day: 'Our dogs are not machines, they all have their own personalities, so it takes time for us to learn how to read them and to fully pre-empt them,' she said. It was no surprise that whenever we went on that route again, Indigo was put on his lead well in advance of arriving at the pony's field!

Drugs in a Pocket?

Indigo continued to settle into my routine at work, both in the office, and at the various locations I had to visit as part of my responsibilities in my role as a probation officer. On one occasion I was due to visit one of my cases in a local prison. He was due to be released later in the year 'on licence.' Being released 'on licence' means that for the remainder of their sentence, the offender must stick to certain conditions and rules. Time spent 'on licence' in the community is supervised by a probation officer who is responsible for developing an appropriate risk management plan. If the licence conditions are broken the released offender may be sent back to prison. I was keen to meet with the prisoner in question so that I could go through his licence conditions and get a sense of the best way to work with him including explaining what he could and could not do when he was released. Building a rapport with the people that we work with is an essential part of the job and one of the rewards for me is the satisfaction I feel when a person has been able to turn their life around and turn their back on criminal behaviour.

It was my first visit with Indigo to HMP Channings Wood. I was familiar with the checking in process although each prison has slightly different entrances. My details were checked and we entered the visits hall to be met by staff who were to pat us down over our clothes giving us a body search. This enables staff to ensure that visitors are not bringing in any banned or contraband items. I had Indigo's treat bag in my pocket to provide rewards for being well behaved. I openly declared it to the prison officer who inspected it and could see it was a bag of dog treats.

She handed them back to me and I slipped them safely back into my pocket. As I turned the corner, I saw that the drug detection dog was in operation on this particular day. The delightful and bouncy Springer Spaniel was circling and sniffing and checking that the row of patiently waiting visitors had no banned items on them. I asked the prison officer who had carried out my body search if she would mind holding onto Indigo whilst I joined them.

The energetic Spaniel started sniffing and with a quick circle around my chair, she firmly pushed her nose under my elbow to indicate to the handler I had something on me. Mortified, I quickly grabbed Indigo's treat bag and declared this to the handler. Satisfied that there was nothing untoward, the handler stated he was happy, and I went back round the corner to fetch Indigo. As I did so, the handler pulled out a ball for the Spaniel as her reward for finding the treat bag.

Quick as a wink, Indigo spotted not only a potential playmate but also a ball to have a play with and started to behave in a very excited manner, pulling on his lead. Clearly, he wanted to join in on a game. I muttered to him: 'No it's not your ball' and feeling somewhat embarrassed, I did my best to look as professional as I could walking up to introduce myself to the prisoner in the open visits' hall. He sat patiently, having observed the whole scenario, and was chuckling away to himself that this eminent professional he was about to meet had a dog with her who just wanted to play. It turned out to be a good way of breaking the ice, and any awkwardness in discussing the restrictions we were placing on him for his impending release was alleviated by the fun of watching a dog who simply wanted to play ball.

Weekend Lie-ins

On workday mornings, I would set my alarm for 6.30am and when it went off, Indigo would diligently put his paws on the bed to alert me that it was time to get up. If Ralph was at home, he would tell me that more often than not, there would be quite a delay between the alarm going off and Indigo alerting me! Sometimes he would first have a little stretch and scratch before the customary paws would reach up to tell me to switch off the alarm. During this time, Ralph would duly pretend to still be asleep so that Indigo could do his job.

At weekends, we often desired a glorious lie-in and not wanting to leap out of bed, I usually set the alarm a bit later so we could make the most of catching up on sleep. However, our pint-sized cat Sooty had other ideas. Instead of letting us lie in quietly, his priority was to get us up so that he could be fed. He had no qualms about telling us this was the case and would start stomping all over us demanding attention. When this did not work and we sleepily shooed him off our heads, Sooty would up the ante. He would walk over to my bedside cabinet and scatter objects onto the floor just near Indigo's bed. This would inevitably leave Indigo feeling insecure as he did not want to be hit by flying objects. As a result, he would use his Hearing Dogs alarm training and put his paws on the bed to get me up. As anticipated, Sooty had manipulated the situation in order to get us to leap out of bed to feed him and all the other animals in the household. It may be possible to fend off a small cat, but 36 kg of agitated Labrador Retriever is a rather more daunting prospect. Sooty was not called the Pint-Sized Peril for nothing.

Easing The Tension

Part of my role as a probation officer involved delivering a domestic violence programme with another colleague. The men attending the programme had been convicted of serious domestic violence and were required to attend a group session every week. The sessions were held in the evening in our group room which could hold approximately 15 of us seated. The group was arranged in a circle so we were facing each other ensuring that everyone could see and no one felt left out.

Our sessions consisted of discussing with the men the behaviours that were abusive. We would probe into their thinking and look at what was going on for them so that they could explore alternative ways to manage their behaviour.

There was often some anxiety within the group at the start of the evening. This was to be expected as the men knew they would be asked to discuss how their week had gone and report any abusive behaviours. They were aware that this would involve gentle probing as we endeavoured to get them to reveal what was going on for them as well as the other participants also holding them accountable for their actions. Although this left the men feeling uncomfortable, having a mirror held up to their behaviours enabled them to start looking at ways they could do things differently.

At the start of one Wednesday session, twelve men arrived, some muscular and heavy set. My colleague Paul and I settled them in the room with coffee and biscuits, and the chairs started to fill up. They had strict instructions not to feed Indigo any of their biscuits and they happily obliged although this did not stop Indigo eyeing the hands that held any biscuits in the hope that they might succumb. Paul and I set up the screen for showing the weeks learning and were chatting with the men to put them at their ease, Indigo settled himself obediently in the middle of the circle.

I sat in my seat and while waiting for everyone to settle, I looked down at Indigo. There amid his black fur was a fully erect pinky penis! I looked up to see that one of the men in the group had also spotted it. His eyes shot an amused smile and he looked at me as though he was about to make a comment. I quickly shook my head and mouthed to him: 'Don't.' Thankfully he made no mention of what he had just witnessed and as I relaxed into my chair, the moment passed but not without a wicked twinkle in the man's eye. It had certainly eased any discomfort this particular man had felt about the evening thanks to Indigo. Mercifully, the evening continued without any further incident.

Bed And Breakfast Volunteers

A few months had passed since Jean's death, and we had made a number of visits to Filey to sort out her house. It was a difficult and harrowing time as with any death that is unexpected. However, Indigo took the travel all in his stride settling on the back seat safely clipped in by his harness. It was with great joy that during this difficult time I had the pleasure of being in contact with Indigo's bed and breakfast volunteers, Jo, and Paul.

The Hearing Dog charity is extremely fortunate in having many wonderful volunteers who support them in various ways. Back when Indigo was training, volunteers who lived near one of the two training centres were able to collect a hearing dog from the kennels on a Friday night and return it to 'school' on a Monday morning. The mutual benefits were that the dogs were able to relax in a calm home environment and the volunteers were able to enjoy having a dog without the commitment of owning one.

During covid, the kennels were closed and all the hearing dogs in training were looked after by the volunteers full-time in their own homes. This was so successful that post covid the kennels have remained closed and all hearing dogs from birth to partnership are looked after and trained by volunteers at home under the guidance and support of the Charity's experienced training staff.

Jo and Paul had relatives who lived in Filey. So, when we told them that we were planning one last visit to Filey it was arranged that we would meet up. When they knocked on the door of Jean's house, Indigo's delight at seeing them again was a joy to experience. Jo and Paul were clearly moved that 'Big D' (their pet-name for him) had not forgotten them. We all realised that Indigo had brought us together and that he had not forgotten the important role they had played in his life. We are still in touch and to this day I have never forgotten the joy of meeting them and how it helped to alleviate some of the painful process for us in saying goodbye to the beautiful town that Jean had lived in for 20 years. It was a beautiful and joyful meeting. They will probably never realise just how much it meant to us both.

Highway Walks

Back to our work routine. I had to make a prison visit to one of my prisoners who had been convicted of a sexual offence. I was accompanied by one of my police colleagues, Jim, a MOSOVO officer. MOSOVO means Manager of Sex Offences and Violent Offences. Jim was great company, a man who had many years of experience in the police and had seen plenty of men on the wrong side of the law. His dry sense of humour was a perfect counter balance in his role hearing some difficult cases over the years.

I looked forward to my joint visits with Jim as I always felt comfortable in his company. I found myself often amused by his wry observations, and yet I also respected his professionalism and judgement when managing our joint cases. This visit to one of the more local prisons, was in an area Jim was familiar with so he happily drove us there.

Jim always ensured that our lunch breaks were taken in areas suitable for Indigo's all-important lunchtime walk. So, we pulled into a service area surrounded by a very pretty woodland copse. After our satisfying lunch, Indigo and I departed for our walk agreeing to meet back at the car. I was pleasantly surprised to find such a scenic walk along a well maintained and accessible pathway in such a remote setting. Once back at the car and whilst securing Indigo back into his seat, I remarked on my observations to Jim. With his usual dry humour, he happily informed me that it was a well-known 'dogging' site! Fortunately, I had not seen any couples compromising themselves.

Dartmoor Prison

I was a regular visitor to several prisons within the local area whilst managing my cases and attending parole hearings. One of these was HMP Dartmoor, a category 'C' men's prison set high on the moor in Princetown. There are four prison security categories. 'A' being the most secure, to 'D' which is an open prison. Prisoners are assigned a category depending on the crime they committed, their violent tendencies, the risk they impose if they escape and their sentences.

Dartmoor prison was built between 1806 and 1809 to hold prisoners from the Napoleonic wars. It has high, imposing granite walls that dominate the area. To access it you drive through some of the wildest terrain of Dartmoor. Both the inside and outside of the prison is uninviting, bleak, and cold, even on the warmest of summer days. This visit was no different. Preoccupied with thoughts about my upcoming parole hearing case, I paid scant attention to Indigo's loose bowel movements at his toilet break just before entering the prison.

Parole hearings are formal affairs and the parole board has a court-like authority that is independent from the Ministry of Justice. In a nutshell, they make a variety of decisions regarding the release of a prisoner, or provide advice to the secretary of state as to whether prisoners on indeterminate sentences are ready to move to an open prison. There are oral hearings that take place in all of the country's prisons, where the prisoner is present and legally represented.

I checked into the reception at Dartmoor and, waited for my prison colleague to fetch me, deep in thought about my recommendations to the panel. On this occasion, I was presenting evidence that the prisoner needed to do more work on understanding why he had committed the offence. It was a particularly harrowing offence involving the rape of a female hitchhiker whom he had picked up. I had argued in my report that his risk was not yet manageable in the community as he needed to complete some programme work exploring his offence and the motivations behind his behaviour.

I was aware that the prisoner did not agree with my decision and knew that his solicitor would provide a counter narrative as to why he should be released at this stage. I was considering how I would provide my evidence and what questions I would likely be asked, when my prison colleague arrived to take me through to the offices where the hearing was to be held.

My colleague was always a positive and welcoming man which was in sharp contrast to the draughty, dank, and cold exterior of the prison. He took me through a number of steel gates, unlocking each with his chunky metal keys, locking them again after us. Indigo took it all in his stride and did not flinch as the metal-to-metal clanks sounded, as the door locked firmly behind us. A sound that I never got used to in all my time visiting prisons. A deep pitch that penetrated through my hearing aids and I would often flinch as the doors touched their harsh metal to metal.

We arrived at my colleagues' office and he happily went off to make a coffee for us. I looked down at Indigo and noticed that he was not settling but frantically circling as if he needed to toilet again. I felt slight panic and realising that I would not be able to sit in a hearing with Indigo needing to toilet! I dashed out of the office, tugging Indigo with me, to find my colleague. I hastily explained that we would need to access the outside space as quickly as possible, or we would end up with a rather unfortunate and smelly accident.

It felt like something out of an old comedy when you see the films being played in a fast forward format. I do not think I have ever seen my colleague move so swiftly to unlock and lock the gates after us so fast. Reaching the nearest piece of grass within the prison grounds, I could sense the relief for Indigo as he immediately squatted and squirted his brown poo. Luckily, I had the foresight to stuff a few poo bags in my pocket for this eventuality. Our return to the office meant going through the same procedure again, unlocking and locking each of the steel gates. I gave an inwardly sigh of relief that I had read Indigo's needs correctly. Happily, the hearing went ahead with Indigo settled by my side and the panel members were none the wiser to the drama that had taken place minutes before.

As I anticipated, the solicitor grilled me on my reasoning not to recommend release. I had the utmost respect for her, doing the best for her client although, I considered that she was not responsible for managing his risk to the public should he be released at this stage. Suddenly Indigo sat upright and laid his paw on my arm. I sensed that this was his cue to let me know he needed to toilet again. The prisoner's solicitor was summing up and so, aware that the proceedings were coming to an end, I did not request a comfort break to the chair. I determined however that we would be leaving the room as fast as we could once the hearing ended!

Thankfully, my colleague willingly obliged again on the multiple unlocking of gates, and we found the previous patch of grass that Indigo was able to use. I thanked my efficient key holding colleague and as I did so, he chuckled and said that it had certainly livened up our hearing that morning. Any nerves either of us had felt that morning were steadied with the drama of ensuring there were no toilet accidents from Indigo. I made my way back to the reception area, and breathed a sigh of relief. Not only had it been a challenging hearing but coupled with being on high alert with Indigo's bowel movements, I knew it would be a parole hearing I would not forget in a hurry.

Hospital Fan Club

Weekends were a glorious break from early workday mornings and after feeding Indigo and the cats, I would usually make a cup of tea for us both to enjoy in bed and then have a sneaky extra hour cuddled under the duvet. One weekend we had been enjoying our lie in when Indigo gave me an urgent nudge with his nose. I had been shaking out the duvet whilst Ralph was in the bathroom. I usually practiced all the sound work with Indigo every morning after breakfast in order to keep his training up to speed, but on this occasion, we had not set off any sounds, so I knew he was trying to tell me something different.

Indigo loved demonstrating his skills in alerting me to sounds and found it all a game but this had a different urgency. Another insistent nudge from Indigo and I asked him 'What is it?' the usual question I ask when he has nudged me and the cue for him to take me to the source of the sound. Off he went, bounding to the bathroom, anxiously looking back to make sure I was following him. I entered the bathroom and there was Ralph, leaning over the sink, blood pouring out of his nose unable to move his head away without making a bloody mess all over the bathroom floor.

It would have been no use for Ralph to call me because I would not have heard him from the other room. Instead, Ralph had called Indigo to come to him and then asked him to: 'Call Gaynor.' In Perfect style, he had come to alert me that Ralph needed my help. Hearing Dogs are trained the 'call' for when other family members are in the house but in another room and need to get the deaf persons attention.

Despite pinching his nose for some time, we could see that the blood pouring out Ralph's nose was not going to stop. We made a phone call to the NHS Helpline, with me holding the phone to Ralph's ear so he could give a muffled response to what was happening, and the paramedics were dispatched. Indigo refused to leave our sides, nuzzling up close to us and constantly checking that we were OK. Once the paramedics took over, they assessed that the bleeding needed medical care at the hospital as it was not going to stop any time soon. It was still early in the morning and as Indigo had not yet had his early morning walk, it was agreed that I would walk Indigo and come to the hospital later to pick Ralph up.

An hour or so later, I arrived at the hospital and walked into Accident and Emergency. Indigo was wearing his smart burgundy uniform which told everyone that he is my hearing dog. I usually find situations such as hospitals daunting. I would try to navigate my way around the long corridors but unable to understand directions from someone who is not speaking clearly often left me lost and in the wrong place. One of the most important advantages of having Indigo by my side in public places such as hospitals is that people are quickly cued in on the need to speak clearly to me. This prevented the hot feeling of embarrassment that I had previously felt when trying to explain that I needed to lipread, especially if I was still unable to understand what they were saying to me. I had lost count of the many times prior to having Indigo when people would look at me strangely or appear angry when they thought I had ignored them and was being rude.

If Ralph was with me, he would intervene and tell people that I had not heard them or would start signing to me so that I was cued in quickly whilst sending a clear message to people of my deafness. Situations like these, when Ralph was in hospital, and I needed to navigate my own way around were much less stressful with Indigo by my side. I need not have worried as when I arrived, I was quickly shown through to the cubicle where Ralph was sitting upright on the bed. The sight would have been comical if I was not so worried about why Ralph had started bleeding so profusely. He had a big wooden peg clamped onto his nose and was holding a cardboard bowl under his chin to catch any bloody drips. He was clearly feeling sorry for himself and informed me that the nurses had popped in every ten minutes or so to check that he was okay and to make sure that the peg was doing its job! It was therefore with some amusement, we found out that word had gone round the department that a lady had arrived with a hearing dog. We suddenly found our little cubicle rather crowded with about five nurses cooing and fussing over Indigo calling him a beautiful boy. I looked on with pride at how Indigo was taking it all in his stride, I glanced up to see Ralph, with his dry sense of humour claiming that no-one was making a fuss of him as he asserted that he was 'Just dying here.' Happily, the peg on the nose had done the job and it appeared that this was just a one-off incident as no further nose bleeds of that type happened again. I do like to think that the hard-working nurses on that day had their morning brightened up with cuddles from my canine partner.

Volunteer Speaker

Each hearing dog partnership is supported by a partnership instructor from the Charity. I started off with Lyndsey, an enthusiastic and supportive lady to whom I felt I could tell everything about my life with Indigo. The partnership instructors are also there if the hearing dog is struggling with aspects of their sound work, or working when in their uniform, or with their general behaviour either in the home or when out and about. They support the partnership suggesting solutions to any problems, and check in every few months to make sure everything is going well.

Lyndsey was aware that I was enjoying my time with Indigo. I had proudly told her about the incident of the nosebleed and how well Indigo had responded when he needed to let me know that Ralph needed me. I had now been with Indigo two years, and Lyndsey informed me that the Charity would be starting community days, which would give us an opportunity to meet other partnerships and volunteers from the Charity. It was with great anticipation that I looked forward to attending the community day to be held at Exeter Deaf Academy in October 2014.

Not only was I looking forward to meeting other partnerships and volunteers, but Lyndsey was aware that through my work I was very confident in public speaking. She asked me if I would be prepared to give a short presentation about how much Indigo had meant to me. I was absolutely delighted to oblige and eagerly put some photos together to make a short presentation, which would include some funny stories, but focus mostly on the difference that Indigo had made to my life.

I arrived in plenty of time on the day and Ralph was happy to join me as it was an invaluable opportunity to meet other partnerships in the local area and gain insight from their experiences. I went to sit at the front so I would not miss my cue to stand up and speak. As it happened, another black Labrador in his hearing dog uniform was also sitting near the front and when we passed, the dog stood up and barked at us both.

Clearly mortified, Helen, the human partner, was trying to calm him down. I was later to find out she had not long been partnered with her hearing dog and one of the things she had been warned about was that her Labrador found other black Labradors a cue to be barked at! It was something Helen was working on, and she was doing her best to sit away from other black Labradors hence why she was sitting on her own at the front. The only person to come and sit near her was me with Indigo, a black Labrador Retriever! We did get to know each other following that day and still laugh about it. Indigo's calm and gentle nature also helped her dog, Sam to overcome his anxiety of other black Labradors and, if they were not on duty in their uniforms, the two dogs would play happily whenever they met up.

The time came to give my talk and there were over a hundred people in the audience. They ranged from partnerships, volunteers and to my delight I spotted the beautiful golden Labrador, Boots from our assessment day. I reflected that Boots was part of my journey in understanding what the reality would be like to always have a dog by your side. I smiled, fondly remembering how petrified I had been going into the supermarket with Boots and taking his lead whilst wheeling a trolley in the store. I realised how far I had come with Indigo and how natural it felt having him next to me when shopping.

I took a deep breath and shared a short story of my life before Indigo, not hearing sounds and the playground story of missing the sound of the whistle when playtime was over. I then shared my photos of being matched with Indigo and our first weekend when we arrived home and the story of Sooty bullying Indigo and sharing the story of Ralph's nosebleed. I finished it off by sharing how I was proud and no longer embarrassed about being deaf, and how having Indigo supported the process of my identity as a deaf person.

The talk went down well, and, many people came up to me afterwards to thank me for sharing my story and giving an insight into what having a hearing dog meant for me. It felt such pride, when one of the Hearing

Dogs' volunteering team asked me if I would be interested in becoming a registered volunteer speaker for the Charity. It was something I was delighted to do as I was fast becoming a passionate advocate of the Charity. I felt it was a skill I could use to give back to them by way of thanks for the gift of being matched with Indigo.

I spent a glorious afternoon, learning the ropes of what information to get across about Hearing Dogs. However, what really resonated with me was that each of us who has a hearing dog has our own personal story of what they mean to us, and that this is the most powerful message we can put across to any audience. It is something I have kept true to ever since when giving any presentations or talks to groups.

The Notorious Smell

My morning routine was to become second nature, practicing sound work around the house, and taking Indigo for his walk before starting the day. Toileting during his early walk is an important part of Indigo's Day, and it ensures he is comfortable before going to work. However, one such morning, he tested my carefully planned timekeeping and routine by reminding me that when he is having his walks off lead, he is first and foremost a dog.

Labrador's have a fantastic sense of smell, and Indigo's nose can sniff out anything new that he might come across from a great distance. However, this particular morning, I think that even he thought on reflection that what he smelt and enjoyed was not perhaps the best decision he could have made. It was a tight schedule that morning, a MAPPA meeting booked. MAPPA means Multi-Agency Public Protection Arrangements and is designed to protect the public, including previous victims of crime, from serious harm by sexual and violent offenders. The meeting requires the local criminal justice agencies and other statutory bodies dealing with offenders to work together in partnership. This ensures agencies share information on an offender so that their risk can be managed in the timeliest way.

I was aware that the meeting was going to be chaired by our local Police Superintendent, who I had the utmost respect for. An energetic, vibrant woman whose knowledge and understanding of managing risks, left me feeling confident that we were working to best practice in managing the risks of any of my cases. In addition, her humility, people skills, and humour were such that you always wanted to do the best you could if she made any requests of you.

Whilst walking, I mentally prepared for the meeting and was suddenly aware that Indigo had trotted off over an embankment, and was out of sight. Conscious that time was ticking on, I pulled out the whistle around my neck and gave three short blasts to recall him back to me. Recall is an imperative signal that tells a trained hearing dog that it should immediately return to its partner. To motivate your dog's immediate response, they are rewarded with a high-level treat such as a piece of cheese or sausage.

Time was of essence. The need to get back to the house in time and get changed out of my walking clothes, into something more respectable for the office. Still out of sight, I whistled for Indigo again. Finally, a reluctant face came out from behind the embankment. He walked slowly up to me, claiming his prized piece of sausage. As he did so, I caught a whiff of something which did not smell pleasant. Not quite the smell of poo, but something equally pungent, although I could not decipher what Indigo had been sniffing. I went to investigate, and climbed up over the embankment. There, lying in the grass, was a dead badger. Decaying in the grass, it looked as though it had been there for some considerable time. I glanced at Indigo and he looked up at me, appearing to be very pleased with himself. Clipping his lead, I hastily pulled him away from the offensive smell. However, the smell continued to follow us. I made the judgement that Indigo had decided to have a good roll in the dead badger. My judgement was correct. As we walked back to the house, I noticed Indigo trying to get away from the smell. I think that even he was having second thoughts on this being the best idea he had of the day!

Luckily, Ralph being with me that morning, we quickly marched Indigo into the garden and filled up a watering can of warm water. I took myself off to find the dog shampoo I had bought for such emergencies. It was only after the third wash of dog shampoo; the smell was not so pungent. However, I was aware that should anyone decide to put their nose too close to his coat of fur, they would get a whiff of something unpleasant. I dashed hurriedly to work and, arriving in the office, I warned colleagues not to sniff him too closely.

It was with relief that our MAPPA meeting went ahead, seamlessly. During the meeting, I detected that even Indigo was showing signs of being fed up with his own smell. Occasionally he would sniff the air, get up, and try to move away from it. I still do not know if that was the result of him sniffing several shampoo rinses, or the dead badger. Thankfully, in the following days on our walk, he showed no signs of wanting to repeat the experience.

Toilet Dramas

In my spare time, I continued to give talks for the Charity and word quickly spread. I was becoming a popular speaker with the local Women's Institute or WI as they are known. I was receiving regular requests to talk to various WI groups and decided to invest in my own projector. This enabled me to connect it to my laptop and show photos and videos of my life with Indigo and, information about the charity. I developed a routine before a talk. Ticking everything off my checklist in preparation for packing the car. This included Indigo's bed and the most importantly, his burgundy uniform, to show him at his best, and demonstrate his very important role, as a hearing dog.

One of my WI evening talks, Indigo had been in the garden with loose bowel movements. The first thing I do when I arrive at a venue, is check whether Indigo needs to toilet. In order to encourage him to toilet, I use the command 'Hurry up.' This is part of the hearing dog's training and upon hearing it, Indigo knows what I am asking him to do. It is especially important when time is of essence such as quick breaks or in this instance, when we were about to go into the hall and give a talk.

Indigo obliged by having a wee and off we went, into the hall, setting up the projector and leaflets. The meeting appeared to be a lively and busy one. A room full of ladies in the audience, happily chatting amongst themselves whilst we set up. Opening the meeting in the traditional way, the ladies sung 'Jerusalem.' Indigo appeared to enjoy the sing-song, and I waited for the introductions to be made. The Chair gave a lovely introduction and I stood up, first, thanking the members for inviting me to their meeting.

Indigo obligingly settled on his bed I had brought with me. However, as I started to speak, he moved to a lady sitting nearest to him. He then placed his paw on her lap, looking up at her. I thought this was not his usual behaviour as in previous talks I had given, he normally settled beautifully on his bed. The lady in question mouthed: 'How adorable,' as he remained sitting, with his paw resting on her lap. I quickly realised that this was a cue. He was trying to tell her or me, something. I was aware from his loose bowel movements earlier; time would be of essence.

A roomful of expectant faces looking at me were waiting to hear my story and, to hear all about the Charity. Sensing Indigo's desperate need to toilet, I could no longer ignore the very clear signals that Indigo was giving. I hastily explained to the ladies, Indigo's earlier loose bowel movements and that I would need five minutes to take him outside. I suggested that they talked amongst themselves as I bolted to the nearest door and out into the car park. Finding some weeds sprouting, the only piece of greenery, I rapidly took his uniform off so he could relieve himself.

Part of the hearing dog's training is that the dogs do not toilet in their uniform. This is in essence so that dogs know when they are working, and do not try and toilet in the middle of a shop, for example. Indigo had been a star; he duly waited for me to get him outside in the car park and take his uniform off. It was with relief; I had read him correctly. We were then able to go back into the hall, and resume my talk.

I explained what had happened and how the dogs are trained not to toilet with their uniform on. It was a very real, and wonderful way to open my talk and explain just how clever a hearing dog can be. Thankfully the talk went ahead without further incident. There were certainly looks of awe from the audience at not only how intelligent Indigo was in his day-to-day sound work, but also his behaviour around toileting.

Working Away From Home

Work continued to be challenging, interesting and no two days were the same. I had a number of long-term prisoners on my caseload. Inevitably they were coming up to their parole hearings and so reports were prepared to assess their suitability to either progress to open prisons or release. Open prisons are often part of the rehabilitation plan for prisoners moving from closed conditions. Prisoners are trusted to complete their sentences with minimal supervision and perimeter security and are often not locked up in their prison cells. Instead, they do purposeful activities throughout the day and have less restrictions on them.

I had one such prisoner that was currently in Wales and I needed to attend his parole hearing. He was nearing the point whereby he was eligible to be transferred to an open prison. However, both myself and the prison probation officer felt he needed to do a bit more work. His legal representative was claiming he had completed all the necessary work and was ready to be moved to open conditions. Knowing this was not going to be an easy hearing, I expected to be cross-examined in detail.

The hearing required me to stay overnight in a bed and breakfast, being an early start in the morning. I was aware that I would need to be alert, rested, and be able to concentrate, rather than worrying about travelling and any potential traffic jams. Using the work systems to book overnight accommodation required a bit of sleuthing from me. As an assistance dog, Indigo has rights to stay in any accommodation regardless of whether it is a dog/pet friendly establishment.

The Equality Act 2010 and the Disability Discrimination Act 1995 require that disabled people have the same access rights to services such as accommodation, restaurants, pubs, and cafes as everyone else. This means that any accommodation I booked, Indigo would be legally entitled to be by my side. Public places have a duty by law not to refuse entry to a disabled person with an assistance dog and if they refuse to do so, can attract fines of up to £3,000.

I diligently put a note informing the booking company about my assistance hearing dog accompanying me. This is part of a courtesy when booking, and for them to inform the accommodation providers in advance. The sleuthing bit of my booking was to ensure that the location I was staying, had somewhere I could toilet Indigo when we arrived in the evening and the next morning. In addition, I made checks on google maps that there were places that were in walking distance of a decent footpath. An important factor for Indigo's routine morning walk so that he will settle for the rest of the working day.

Planning was an important factor as I knew that without a robust walk in the morning, I would not have a settled dog. I was to travel to the quaint and beautiful town of Usk. I had checked, and decided to book a pub that was in striking distance of the river Usk. I figured that a walk down by the river would be just what we both needed before a long day ahead of us. In addition, I could see that the pub welcomed dogs in the bar, so I felt assured that we would receive a warm welcome when we arrived.

On the day, I had a clear drive and when I arrived in Usk I decided to check the journey time from where I was staying to the prison. Confident that I knew where I was going the following morning and my timings, I drove to the pub and parked up. Pulling out my overnight bag from the boot, I popped Indigo's smart uniform on. Walking into the pub with Indigo, I spotted another dog in the bar and plenty of dog water bowls available. I felt that the canine partners were well catered for and it lifted my heart with pleasure.

My lightness of heart quickly dissipated after explaining to the landlord that we had a booking for the night. I was met with a hostile glare and told that dogs were not allowed in the accommodation. Holding my nerves and ground, I explained that I had put a note on my booking form. I had informed the company I would be bringing an assistance dog. I also quoted the Equality Act and mentioned that they would be breaking the law by refusing my stay. It felt a heart stopping moment. The air between us rested on whether they would continue their stance and refuse my stay.

The landlord told me that they had not been informed of this and there was no such note their end on the booking form. I brought out my little yellow identification book which I always carried with me, to show him. It is provided to all hearing dog partnerships should there be a necessity to explain the law and our assistance dogs when access rights are refused. As I did so, I felt the tension in the air was palpable. My mind did a quick mental check on whether I could find another bed for the night at such late notice. Not something I was relishing. I was not familiar with the town or layout; everyone was a stranger to me and, it was getting late in the day. It was added stress that I did not want to have to deal with on top of what I knew, was going to be a taxing day at work, the next day.

The landlord mumbled that their own dogs were not allowed in their pub accommodation. I calmly explained that Indigo was not a pet. It was to my relief, the landlord reluctantly relented. I thanked them, and informed them that I would like to book a table that evening in the bar, for food. As I was shown upstairs, I gratefully clicked the latch on the door of our room. Alone with just my thoughts and Indigo, I sunk down on one of the comfortable chairs in the room. As I did so, tears of relief trickled down my cheeks. The tension in my body had been intense. It was only behind closed doors that I allowed my tears. They were a safety valve that I could finally release. It was at that moment, my gorgeous canine partner's face peered up at mine, and there, Indigo just loving me unconditionally. Licking away my tears, he realised things had just got a bit too much for his human.

Pampered Pooch

The experience at Usk was behind me and to my delight, in complete contrast to another booking I made at a hotel in Tavistock, some months later. Two days of training was scheduled in Plymouth, and a colleague and I decided that we would join forces and travel together. I had done my usual sleuthing and discovered that the B&B's were all in central urban Plymouth and therefore not suitable for toileting and walking Indigo each day. I looked for an alternative local location and found, to my delight, a hotel advertising as dog friendly, in Tavistock. It was also conveniently located next to a park.

Whilst Indigo has the rights to go to any hotel, battling with unsympathetic proprietors takes steel. Negotiating my rights with a hotel is wearing, coupled with demanding days of training. In my training sessions, I have my portable induction loop system which enables me to hear the trainer clearly. The trainer and I wear small boxes around our necks which means that sounds are transmitted through my hearing aid. This enables me to hear with clarity, the trainer's speech; essential when I am learning something new.

Despite this, it takes a great deal of concentration to hear everything being said and often, by the end of the day, I am tired and exhausted. Booking my accommodation in plenty of time for the training, I informed my colleague the name of the hotel so she could book the same place. Unfortunately, the work system only enabled me to place my own booking. My colleague had to book hers, for herself. Unfortunately, due to workloads, by the time she was able to access the booking site a few days later, there were no longer rooms available at the same hotel in Tavistock. Instead, she secured a room in central Plymouth, within walking distance of the training venue.

The plan on day one of our training was to travel early to Plymouth, complete the days training and then book into our respective accommodation. We would meet up the next day at the training venue and would travel back home together at the end of the last session. All our carefully timed plans were executed on day one. After parting company, I drove with Indigo to our hotel in Tavistock.

Once parked, I made use of the local park for Indigo to toilet before checking into the hotel. As we approached the reception desk, with Indigo resplendent in his smart burgundy uniform, I felt relief to be met with smiles and lots of admiration for Indigo. Check in completed, we headed to our room and unlocking the door, I discovered, on the table, an incredible hamper of goodies. They were not, I discovered on unwrapping them, for me, but for Indigo. Tasty dog treats, a bowl, toy and even a thoughtful roll of doggy poo bags.

I chuckled out loud and Indigo sensing something good was coming his way, sat, eyes wide in anticipation. I gave him a chew which he contentedly chomped on atop his bed whilst I put the kettle on for my much-needed cup of tea.

The rest of the stay continued in the same vein. Feeling rather guilty that my poor suffering colleague was staying in a very basic bed and breakfast, I snaffled some extra pains au chocolate and croissants from the buffet breakfast the next day for her to enjoy at our coffee break.

When I arrived for day two of our training, my suspicions were right that my colleague's breakfast had been barely edible. I showed off the photos of Indigo's wonderful hamper and unwrapped the prized breakfast goodies that I had stowed away. My colleague expressed her gratitude for the wrapped continental breakfast, and shared my wonderment about how much Indigo had been spoilt. It was a memorable stay and one that had been in sharp contrast to the stay I had previously experienced in Usk.

Brownies and Demonstration Dog

In my spare time, I continued to give a number of hearing dog charity talks to organisations. I particularly enjoyed talking to Brownies and schools. Humour is very important to me and I love using it as a tool to get my message across. This is around the difficulties associated with every day communication for deaf people. Ahead of the talks, I would ask the leader if there was a diversity badge that the children were working towards, and if I could help realise this for them.

On one occasion, a group needed to demonstrate they could communicate effectively with a deaf person. After I had shown my Hearing Dogs slide show and taught the children to do the alphabet in sign language, I found a very receptive audience. There was much laughter as they learnt to sign and sing: 'How much is that doggy in the window?' Settling them all down, I proceeded to take out a cup and saucer from my bag and set up a mock café to set the scene. Telling the children that they had spotted me in a café, they wanted to come and talk to me. However, first, they needed to get my attention. There was no shortage of willing volunteers and a funny half hour ensued. The children using hand gestures, tapping me on the shoulder, and signing 'hello' to get my attention, with me replying 'Oh hello,' in a rather affected voice.

I was also delighted that Indigo helped one of the Brownies get over her fear of dogs. The leader informed me that she had a Brownie who was terrified of dogs. However, the Brownie, was able to observe Indigo's gentle calm nature and with the support of her friends, felt confident enough to approach him. She gently placed her hand on his back to stroke him and Indigo, sensing that she was nervous, stayed quiet and still. I swelled with pride when the leader told me that every week, they awarded a Brownie doll which could be kept for week, and was given to an individual girl for doing something outstanding. The nervous young girl who had the courage to come and stroke Indigo had won the doll for that week; such was the magic that Indigo had spun.

After I had been conducting these talks for several months, my partnership instructor became aware of how popular they had become. The Hearing Dogs charity were receiving a significant number of requests from other groups which had heard how enjoyable and fun my talks were. It was 2014 and I had been with Indigo for a couple of years now.

An email arrived in my inbox from the head office for hearing dogs, outlining a new scheme the charity was setting up. Using ambassador dogs for demonstrating at talks, the demand for them to attend talks was outstripping the number of available dogs. There were not enough dogs that were sufficiently trained, and more importantly, confident enough to demonstrate sound work in front of an audience. The email asked if I would be interested in learning how to use Indigo to demonstrate when I gave talks. I was delighted, and quickly emailed back to register my interest.

What followed was a gorgeous day at the headquarters in Buckinghamshire, learning how to set up the sounds. These were the cooker timer, smoke alarm and the 'call' to show how Indigo worked for me. There were six of us, Indigo being the only Labrador Retriever in the group, the others being poodles and cocker spaniels. The trainer had her own retired demonstration hearing dog who was still happily showing the trainee demonstration dogs the ropes. She talked us through setting up the sounds, but also impressed upon us that the most important part, that the well-being of the dogs was paramount, and, that they remained happy showing their sound work in front of an audience.

Having shown us how to set up the cooker timer with her dog, the trainer asked for willing volunteers using our own dogs in front of the class. Noticing that the others were more hesitant, I volunteered to go first. Setting up the cooker timer on a low table, I confidently put a treat next to the timer and showed Indigo what I had done. I asked Indigo to wait in between me and the timer. The timer pinged its sound and Indigo duly got up, walked over to me, and nudged me confidently on my leg. As soon as

I said: 'What is it?' he trotted over to the timer and waited for me to hand him his treat.

The others were full of admiration. They exclaimed that their dogs would have already eaten the treat that I had precariously placed by the timer well within reach of a canine mouth. I swelled with pride at my boy, he had not let me down. Completing the routine beautifully, it was an exciting moment. Indigo was now a demonstration dog, this meant I could now show him in action, to groups. It added an extra dimension to the talks I was giving.

The Missing Hot-Cross Bun

Work remained challenging and interesting. Many of my work colleagues appeared to be delighted when Indigo came to break up their day whilst they sat at their desks. One of my colleagues, Julie, would keep her bag under her desk and sometimes leave it overnight, picking it up the next day. Julie's desk was next to where I checked in and out at reception during the day.

We had a system in Devon whereby we would have a board with counters which we swiped when we were in or out of the office. That way, colleagues could see if you were in or not. It was an essential piece of information, especially if service users had popped in requesting to see a particular member of staff. Additionally, colleagues would know who was in the office should they need information. I was working late one night and there were still a few of us in the office, burning the midnight oil so to speak.

Some colleagues were still seeing service users and I had seen the last of mine for the day, and was packing up to go home. I walked down to reception to check myself out. Now that Indigo was so familiar with our routine, he was unclipped from his lead and wearing only his hearing dog coat. In the reception area, I moved my counter over on the board to show I was out of the office. As I did so, I looked down at Indigo to see his nose buried deep in Julie's bag. Quickly telling him to: 'Leave,' he sheepishly brought his nose up, but I could see he had something in his mouth.

Indigo's mouth remained clamped shut as I commanded once again to: 'Leave' whatever it was he had. I quickly dropped my bags and went over to him. He sneakily moved his head away, with his mouth still firmly clasped shut. As I gently held his head, prised open his mouth, there, lodged whole and still intact, was a pilfered hot cross bun. Pulling it out, I placed it on a piece of tissue with a note to my colleague.... 'Dear Julie, I found the pack of your hot cross buns in your bag, and I snaffled one. Mum was not too happy with me and took it out of my mouth which was a shame, I was enjoying it so much. She has placed it here on this tissue. I don't think you will want to eat it now, it's a bit soggy. Mum has told me that we will be going out first thing tomorrow to buy fresh hot cross buns for you. Yours in Paws, Indigo'

The next morning as we walked into the office, carrying a fresh packet of hot cross buns, there was a lot of hilarity emanating from the reception area. Indigo had clearly thought he was the star of the laughter, merrily wagging his tail at everyone chuckling at him. I was pleased to see that Julie's bag was kept well out of his reach that morning!

Celebrity Ambassador

I enjoy living life to the full, trying new things, and I have a curiosity for life which helps me unwind from my busy and complex working environment. I am an ardent reader, loving the joy of losing myself in the written world of books. It was with a great sense of anticipation the annual book festival was arriving, in the North Devon town of Appledore. The pretty harbour town lends itself well to welcoming several well-known authors, making the best use of the village halls and the churches within the town.

When the calendar of talks came out, I earnestly scanned the listings to see who was coming to talk about their books. Having Indigo with me created no impediment to my full enjoyable engagement with the festival. Turning up early to an event enabled me to secure a seat at the front or an aisle where Indigo could lie safely by my feet, not presenting a trip hazard. I had never forgotten my training, the week I spent with Indigo at BWC, learning how to work with him. A big responsibility in a partnership is to ensure that your dog is in a safe place, and does not cause obstructions in public places.

During the 2015 Appledore Book Festival, I saw with great excitement that Pam St. Clement was one of the guest speakers. For 26 years Pam played one of Britain's most iconic soap characters, Pat Butcher in EastEnders. Pam had, and continues to remain a huge supporter and amazing ambassador for hearing dogs for deaf people. She was coming to talk about her newly released book, 'The End of an Earring.'

The talk was to be held in one of the churches in Appledore, one of the larger venues, catering for a big audience. I was also relieved to see that the church had a hearing loop system installed. A hearing loop (sometimes called an audio induction loop) is a special type of sound system for use by people with hearing aids. Providing a magnetic, wireless signal, which is picked up by the hearing aid when set to the 'T' (Telecoil) setting. The hearing loop consists of a microphone to pick up the spoken word; an amplifier which processes the signal which is then sent through the final piece; the loop cable, a wire placed around the perimeter of a specific area i.e., a meeting room, a church, a service counter etc acts as an antenna that radiates the magnetic signal to the hearing aid. I found it a brilliant piece of equipment to enhance my ability to hear.

I persuaded Ralph to join me and to arrive early for the talk, securing that important seat at the front. The seats were allocated on a first come, first serve basis. Whilst there was a loop system, I still needed to be able to see the speaker so I could lip-read. I was aware that if we did not turn up early enough there would be a high chance that the only available seats would be in the middle of the pew, not ideal, as Indigo would not be able to settle comfortably.

Walking to the church entrance, I saw that we were one of the first to arrive. The ushers kindly allowed us to sit on one of the pew seats at the front. After a few minutes sat on the hard wooden pew, Ralph remarked that it was an effective way of reminding the Church audience of the suffering they could expect if they ever ended up in purgatory. I am sure anyone will attest, sitting for any length of time on wooden pews ends up with a rather numb bottom!

I settled Indigo down next to me on the spacious carpet lining the central aisle. Sat at the front meant that no one needed to clamber over him to get to their seat. The only person who would be walking past him would be Pam herself when she arrived. I excitedly did some people watching as we waited for the talk to start. It was with a sense of pride that several people spotted Indigo, gave me warm and appreciative looks, and mouthed how handsome he looked. I smiled enthusiastically back.

The church hall was filled to capacity, and I estimated that there must have been a few hundred people sitting in the audience. The big moment arrived. Pam was escorted along the aisle by Judi Speirs, a radio and television presenter who was to conduct the interview. As they slipped past us, Pam spotted Indigo. A broad smile swept across her face. She mouthed that she loved the Charity. Taking their place on the stage, we all enjoyed an insightful and interesting hour of how Pam came to write her book. She shared snippets of her time spent in the area of Dartmoor as a child, and her inspiration when writing.

The hour whizzed by and there was an opportunity at the end of the talk to ask questions. I could not resist asking a question and eagerly put my hand up. Waiting for the microphone to be passed to me, I was thinking on my feet about the way I would frame my question. As I took the microphone, I realised that by sitting at the front, not everyone behind me would have spotted Indigo lying by my side. I started my question by introducing the fact that Indigo, my assistance hearing dog was with me, and that Pam was involved in the Charity as an ambassador.

Getting into my groove of public speaking, I said that Indigo meant the world to me and that I wanted to thank her for the work she did for the Charity. I then asked my question which was 'What made you get involved with Hearing Dogs and not another animal charity?' Judi looked across at me and mouthed: 'Great question;' putting both her thumbs up.

Pam explained how she was attending Crufts one year when one of the founding members asked her if she had heard of the charity, Hearing Dogs. She talked about how she marvelled at how a deaf person is supported by the trained dogs. Speaking about the origins of the Charity, she explained that in the beginning, homeless dogs were used and trained to help a deaf person. She believed this was such an amazing charity that she quickly decided to become an active supporter and advocate for their work.

Pam must have talked about the Charity for at least half an hour, sharing how the dogs were trained, and the difference they make to a deaf person's life. It was with some amusement I noted the audiences' reaction, nearing the end of her talk, revealing the £40,000 it costs to fund each hearing dog for a lifetime. There was a collective gasp from the audience and at that moment, all eyes were on Indigo. I sensed that they were looking at him in a different light! It was a magical moment and one that I will always treasure. So many people who may not have been aware of the charity, heard first-hand, from such a well-known and respected celebrity.

Chocolate Labrador

I have always been an avid reader of the local news. One story that piqued my interest was about a new shop owner, Jeannette, taking on a local chocolate shop in Ilfracombe. She had inherited a full-size model of a person made in chocolate, and she was creating a full-size chocolate dog to go with it. Her idea was to have a 'man's best friend, dog,' walking alongside her chocolate person. The article talked about her wanting a name for the dog, and she invited readers to send in their suggestions.

Not wanting to miss an opportunity to do a bit of publicity for the Charity, I put an email together explaining how much Indigo meant to me. Informing her that the dog she was creating was similar size to Indigo, I suggested she might like to name her dog after mine? Receiving a lovely response from Jeannette, the rather apt name of Coco had been chosen. However, she asked me to go and visit her at her shop as she was willing to do some publicity and fundraising for the Charity.

You can imagine that it did not take me long to beat a path to the door of a chocolate shop! Armed with leaflets and a collection tin to display around the dog, I had asked if she would like one of Indigo's old hearing dog coats to put on her chocolate dog. Thinking this would be a good focus point for the Charity, I checked with the marketing team from Hearing Dogs. They confirmed they were happy for me to do this, and were delighted for the publicity.

Jeannette said she was happy to oblige. I spent a delightful hour chatting with her, and setting up the leaflets and collection pot. Of course, I was also surrounded by her delicious hand-made chocolates and I needed little convincing to purchase copious quantities of these essential supplies! She made nearly all the chocolates on the premises, and I was literally a kid in a truly gorgeous sweet shop. Indigo behaved impeccably and even posed next to Coco, the chocolate dog, without even licking him.

Needless to say, I was on a high telling my colleagues the story and the cunning excuse for stocking up on so much chocolate. It is a wonderful testimony to Jeannette that Coco, with his hearing dog jacket, can still be found in her chocolate shop in Ilfracombe today, fundraising for Hearing Dogs for Deaf People.

A New Chapter Awaits

It was in 2015 that we made a big decision that it was time for us to downsize our house. Unfortunately, the best made plans do not always take a straight path. It was 2017 before we were to receive an offer on our house. Two years of maintaining a house constantly ready for potential buyers to view, was taking its toll. We decided we were not going to delay a moment longer when we received an offer. It was an offer that was significantly under our asking price. Work was also beginning to take its toll and added to the level of stress. My working environment had been significantly impacted by the reforms of Transforming Rehabilitation.

Chris Grayling, the then Secretary of State for Justice, had decided that as of June 2014, he would privatise parts of the Probation Service. The reforms replaced 35 publicly-owned Probation Trusts with a National Probation Service (NPS) and 21 privately-owned Community Rehabilitation Companies (CRCs). The former was to manage offenders who posed a high risk of harm to the public; the latter to supervise low-to-medium risk offenders. A 'Payment by Results' mechanism was introduced to remunerate private providers, the stated aim of which was to facilitate 'innovative' practice.

In the run up to these reforms, the Probation Unions were in contentious discussions. A number of strikes were held in an attempt to try to convince the Government to change their mind, sadly without success. Trying to make money out of the management of offenders would be an unmitigated disaster. In addition, valued and experienced probation officers were either leaving the service or were spilt into the two factions. I had been assigned into the National Probation Service under the Ministry of Justice.

My caseload changed overnight. Whereas before the changes, my caseload contained offenders of differing levels of risk, now all the men I was supervising were deemed a high risk of harm to the public. It was relentless. The impact on morale, coupled with the additional stress caused by the cultural shift of the service and long hours, started to have an impact. We both felt the time was right to consider the offer on our house. Having taken this important decision, we could start to imagine what new adventures and opportunities might be opened to us.

Ralph had googled possible places for us to live in the UK that we could afford. To our complete surprise, the search revealed an area in Cumbria. Having loved the Lake District on previous visits with its awesome mountains and lakes, we decided it was a serious contender. Spending a glorious week house hunting, we found our desired location and bungalow. It was an exciting time. I gave in my resignation at work and realised a lot of colleagues were genuinely shocked when I told them our news. It was the first time we had considered a move from the area.

We started to pack up our lives ready for the new adventure and my last day in the Devon office was fast approaching. I was called down into the manager's office to find my colleagues all gathered around for a farewell speech and presentation. I was quickly reminded of just how big a part Indigo had played in all my colleagues' lives. His presence and friendly nature had cheered up their working days. His customary daily visits and demanding strokes, would lift their spirits if they were feeling down. He was held in such high regard and had been fully accepted as a member of the probation team. Everyone in the office had been touched by this unique member of staff, in one way or another. Emotions were kept in check when I was told of course they would miss me. However, I was left in little doubt that Indigo was considered to be the most important member of our little team. I chuckled out loud when sternly told not to get too excited with all the gifts bought by my colleagues. Most of them were not for me, but for Indigo. As usual, his nose sensed which gifts were for him as I opened the thoughtful presents. A ball, treats and yet more treats for Indigo. I too had not been forgotten and was spoilt. Amongst my beautiful gifts, one of the team had been dispatched off to Ilfracombe Chocolate Emporium to buy the most glorious box of chocolates for me. It was a delightful send-off!

Canoeing the Lakes

The Lakes awaited us. We arrived on a dark, overcast day in November 2017. The first six months in our new home, in the town of Millom, were taken up with the renovation of our bungalow, and getting to know the local area. A new partnership instructor from hearing dogs was assigned to me, now living in a different location. Andy arrived not long after we moved in. He saw that Indigo and I have a very strong bond, now having been a partnership for five years. He was satisfied that we were doing everything correctly by the way we worked instinctively together.

As we explored the glorious Lake District through the Spring and Summer, we realised how much we loved the water. We decided that it would be fun to try out a canoe. We had rented a kayak in Devon and had bought Indigo his own life jacket. However, whilst we coaxed him on the kayak, splashing along the coastline with its choppy waves, he made it known to us that he was not very keen. The kayak was not very stable for a 36kg dog. Back on the sandy shore, he would not come near us, fearing we would put him back on it. We realised that the kayak was not going to work. However, whilst on holiday in the Lakes a few years previously, he had enjoyed a trip on a rowing boat.

We anticipated that the stability of a canoe might give him enough confidence to be comfortable on the water with us. We booked a lesson on how to paddle safely, steer and get out of trouble should we capsize and made the decision to buy our own canoe. Our first outing with Indigo in tow was a joy. Not spending too long on the first session, we gradually built-up Indigo's confidence. We did not want to repeat the kayaking experience. Our calculation proved correct. Indigo quickly adapted to the canoe. He soon began to actively look forward to our adventures on the lake, his tail wagging enthusiastically if he spotted us loading the canoe on the top of our car.

Canoeing was to be a fabulous experience. The canoe enabled us to have glorious days out on the Lakes. Indigo sat in between my legs at the back, surveying the land and water, looking very regal. Gliding through the stunning Lakes of Coniston, Ennerdale and Windermere, the looks from people on the shore were mostly of smiles and chuckles. We could see they would do a double take when they spotted our third crew member. A dog in a life jacket. Looking as he did, every part the coxswain of the canoe.

Indigo's delight at being in the water is often very vocal, emitting high pitched squeaks of delight as he spots a duck or swan swimming near us. He takes great pleasure watching the world go by. On one occasion, we had carried the canoe to the shore of Coniston and Ralph was returning to the car to fetch the last of our essential picnic. A coach party of tourists had just arrived. I put Indigo's life jacket on him, and heard gasps of surprise, some of the party asking if they could take photos of him next to the canoe. I happily obliged and just to show him off, asked him to: 'sit' next to the canoe. We could hear voices raised in admiration as they observed an elegant Indigo, looking every part the captain, of our little canoe.

Ralph returned with the rest of our picnic. We carried out our usual routine. This would begin with me, clambering into the canoe first, and then it was Indigo's turn. Once he was settled in his favourite position, between my knees at the stern, Ralph pushed us out a bit further and clambered in. It was a relief it had gone to plan. We looked as though we were seasoned pros in front of our audience. As we elegantly sliced through the waters, the sound of cameras could be heard merrily clicking away.

Crufts Here We Come

Changes were afoot in the probation service. In May 2019, the Conservative Government revealed that the National Probation Service would reassume responsibility for the day-to-day management of all offenders. Dame Glenys Stacey, the-then Chief Inspector of HMI Probation, called Transforming Rehabilitation 'Irredeemably flawed.'

It was therefore no surprise, that the prior warnings from experienced probation professionals, portrayed by the Government as doomsayers, had all come to pass. I kept an eye on the developments and started to feel that my experience could be put to good use again. My time out from the service had left me feeling refreshed, restored, and resolute that I would strike a better work/life balance.

It was with this in mind; I contacted an agency enquiring if there were any local jobs in the probation service, where my skills set could be used. In many ways, I should not have been surprised that in the space of an hour, I received five different people contacting me from the agency. They outlined all the jobs that were available. One of the emails asked: 'Would you be interested in a part time role as a probation officer in the local prison?' I duly started the paperwork to initiate the process.

Whilst the paperwork was going through, I met with Andy again to complete our yearly progress report. This was to ascertain how Indigo was settling into his new home. As we were chatting, Andy asked if I would be interested in representing the Charity at Crufts in 2019. It was rather a lovely surprise to be asked. Hearing dogs were planning to set up a stand at Crufts. They wanted a rota of partnerships with their dogs, to be on the stand for a couple of hours.

I did not want to miss this wonderful opportunity. I asked Andy to put my name forward for consideration. Due to the distance, I offered to do a couple of slots over two days. It was with great excitement when I received the news that my offer was accepted. I made plans for the trip and booked an overnight stay at a local hotel near the NEC.

The scale of the show is impressive. I was amazed to see so many dogs related goods and services for sale, as well as all the competitions for various skills such as agility and obedience. I had fun spotting the celebrities and with my camera on hand, Clare Balding and her filming crew kept popping up in my eye line.

To be part of the Hearing Dogs stand was great fun. At one end of the display stand was a big wheel stating it was the 'Wheel of Pawtune.' Visitors could pay to spin the big wheel and whichever dog picture the arrow landed on; they would win a prize. It was so imaginative and a great talking point, opening up conversations with the public. The rest of the stand was thoughtfully planned with a short white picket fence around the perimeter of the allocated area. Within the fence, there was mock grass and benches where Hearing Dog recipients chatted to the public about the difference our partnership dogs made to our lives.

There were some familiar faces with the burgundy team on the stand. The 'burgundy team' is an affectionate name which the volunteer family use, owing to the colour of our T-shirts. These match the hearing dog uniform. One particular face, I felt I knew, but could not place. As we got chatting, I found to my delight, she worked as a partnership instructor and was based in Wales. When I asked her if she also completed assessments for newly placed dogs, she confirmed she did. The penny dropped! She was my assessor when Indigo had decided to run off and bark at the Dartmoor pony.

The stern face with the clipboard was nowhere to be seen. Smiling back at me, I could see a warm, friendly, and approachable lady. I reminded her that we had previously met for Indigo's assessment. I explained how mortified I was that Indigo had misbehaved. She chuckled. She did indeed remember me. Assuring me I was not alone when our dogs did not 'perform' on their assessment days. It was a delightful reunion and, there was more to come.

I had been in communication via social media with Lisa, partnered with Indigo's sister, Inca. I told Lisa that Indigo and I were going to Crufts and asked if she also planned to go. Not wanting to pass up the opportunity to meet, she made plans to stay at the same hotel where we were staying. Indigo and Inca not only were brother and sister but as is customary in the Charity, when a litter is born, the Charity name all the litter with the same letter.

Indigo and Inca were part of a litter of eight puppies. Their names all began with the letter 'I.' Ivor and Isla were also part of the litter, and I was aware that they were working as hearing dogs, in other parts of the country. It was exciting knowing I was going to meet one of Indigo's siblings. My anticipation grew. Lisa messaged me on my phone, informing me she had arrived at the Crufts Hall. It was my allocated slot on the Hearing Dogs stand. I waited keenly to see if Indigo would recognise his sister.

When Lisa and Inca arrived, I realised that it was us humans more excited for the meet. Indigo and Inca gave a customary sniff in each other's direction. They clearly looked very comfortable sitting next to each other. My allocated hour came to an end and I shared with Lisa that I was going to make my way to the hotel to take Indigo for a walk and freshen up. Planning to meet up later for drinks and a meal with Lisa's husband in tow, it was a fabulous end to the day. I had a very memorable evening with Lisa. We shared our experiences of the daily struggles of being deaf and the magic of being partnered with a hearing dog.

If I thought the two days could not get any better, I was mistaken. At breakfast the next morning, I was enjoying the delights of the buffet breakfast when my eyes were drawn to another assistance dog sitting nearby. The dog was wearing a jacket stating it was a hearing dog/dual assistance dog. His owner sat at the table in a wheelchair and was accompanied by her partner who was fetching the food from the buffet table.

I had finished my breakfast and not wanting to pass up an opportunity for a chat, I went over to her table and introduced myself. Explaining to her that I gave a lot of talks for the Charity, I was able to talk about what Indigo does for me. However, I wanted to know exactly what her dog did for her. She was clearly delighted to share with me the work her dog was able to do. She described her daily routine. Her dog alerted her to all the sounds in the same way Indigo did. However, she needed some extra support with regards to her wheelchair usage.

She told me that in her house were ropes all around the handles of the doors. Her dog was trained to pull the ropes, to open the doors. In addition, her dog could pull out her clothes from her washing machine. Then she came to the bit that absolutely blew my mind. When she was out and about shopping, her dog was trained to jump up and activate the push pad on shops with his paws. This automatically opened the door. I told her I was astounded, delighted to meet with her, and listen to the difference her dog made to her life. I assured her that she had given me an extra dimension that I would share in my future talks about how life changing our hearing dogs are for us.

Crufts had been a truly rewarding experience. I was indebted to the Charity for inviting me to be with the team on the Hearing Dog stand. As I drove away after completing my second stint on the stand, I reflected on how grateful I was to have been matched with Indigo. He had given me such a positive deaf identity. However, my high spirits were soon to be brought down to earth, with an almighty crash.

Reality Check

I required a break at one of the motorway service stations. Indigo and I needed a toilet, and I wanted to top up with some much-needed caffeine. I ensured Indigo was toileted first, then I made my way to the entrance and to use the facilities. As I walked towards the shop, there stood an imposing security guard. He approached me and was looking at us both, saying something to me. I could not fully hear what he was saying but I second guessed he was refusing my entrance with Indigo into the shop.

Patiently, I explained to him the Equality Act 2010 and that my assistance dog had the same rights as guide dogs for the blind. I thought that was the end of it. I wandered into the shop, but the guard decided to follow me and at the same time, kept talking to me. Not only did this become quite threatening but I had no idea what he was saying to me. I ended up telling him to go and fetch his manager if he did not believe what I was saying.

He stopped following me; but kept a watchful eye on me the whole time whilst I was browsing in the shop. The experience was really distressing. As well as feeling stressed and flustered, I found it hard to concentrate on what I had originally wanted to buy. I came out of the shop feeling really stressed, upset and close to tears. It was a stark reminder to me that when access is challenged or denied, it is really upsetting.

My experience of being told I cannot enter with a hearing dog is thankfully not a daily occurrence. When it does happen, it is not only a case of having to educate people, it is also a matter of having to summon up the courage to stand my ground. This can be hard on top of the exhausting effort it takes to hear and understand what people are saying. It was in such stark contrast to the amazing two days I had enjoyed at Crufts.

Indigo Weaves his Magic

During this time, my application to work at the prison was still being processed, all my security passes were now ready. It was June 2019 and I was to start as a probation officer in the local prison. As I expected, it was a very different culture to the one I had known in the community. I had no concerns that Indigo would not be looked after. The head of the department ensured that there were extra bowls and a big bed for him should I need to work in different locations around the prison.

Indigo was his usual supportive self. After a particularly difficult day trying to juggle my caseload and frustrated that there were simply not enough hours in the day, I sat in my line manager's office and burst into tears. It was a tense moment as my poor manager was not quite sure what to do with my sudden release of pent-up emotions. Indigo on the other hand was an accomplished master at managing his partners' different moods. He started pulling at my shoe, trying to steal it off my foot. We both laughed and immediately it eased the tension. We then were able to calmy talk about what could be done to ensure I could meet all my targets.

Working with the prisoners was not so different to being in the community. I was interested in their stories and endeavoured to build a rapport with the men. I wanted to assist them in completing their integration back into the community. However, there were some hard-to-reach prisoners, and I had been assigned to one such man; *Mike*. A long-term prisoner having served over twenty years in prison. During my first meeting with *Mike*, he admitted that he struggled to trust professionals. He sat with his arms crossed, viewing me suspiciously, with a scowl on his face.

Indigo sensed something in *Mike*. He happily trotted over to him and allowed himself to be stroked. Something shifted over a few sessions. *Mike* would enjoy making a fuss of Indigo and stroke him. He divulged that all through his life he had been let down by numerous people. He told me that the one thing he knew to be true, that animals were not going to hurt him. At the start of each session, he would sit himself on the floor to make a fuss of Indigo. It was to be a positive dynamic as I sat on the floor with them both, drawing out *Mike's* story.

Indigo enjoyed the fuss *Mike* made of him and sensed he needed some affection. It was something I perceived that he had been deprived of, most of his life. He was willing to open up more about his life experiences, and shared his hopes and fears for the future. He has moved onto another prison now, although I always like to think that Indigo played a part in helping *Mike* on his journey. I hope he started to trust humans a bit more and to a greater extent, work with professionals in a positive way.

Virtual Talks

The year was now 2020 and around the world COVID was beginning to have an impact on everyone's lives. Staff in prisons were deemed essential workers although our meetings with the men were somewhat restricted. If we could work from home, we were encouraged to do so. In every organisation, new ways to work remotely were quickly initiated. It was no different for the Hearing Dogs Charity. Our live talks stopped, and instead virtual zoom talks became the new normal.

It was an interesting way to deliver a talk and, for a deaf person it presented its own challenges. It also meant that distance was no longer an obstacle. We were just a mere click away from joining in with a group, all around the country. I started to work out a methodology for how I could deliver a talk remotely. I was mindful that Indigo was an integral part of my talk and devised ingenious ways to show him to those in the audience.

I was using the platform zoom on a laptop. This gave me some flexibility for where I could sit. I set up my first talk on a lounge chair with Indigo sitting by my feet. I thought that this might be the best position for the audience to see him. However, halfway through the talk, Indigo got bored and wandered off to lie on his comfortable bed. I found that I was straining my back to see the audience. I wanted to see how they were reacting to my talk, and needed to lip read any questions. By the end of the session, I found myself with a stiff back.

I quickly realised I would need to change this methodology. Using a straight back dining room chair enabled me to see the screen more easily. After the group leader introduced me, I was able to explain why it was easier for me not to have Indigo on the screen all the time. However, I would build up the expectation that I would show Indigo. First, I explained his breed, his age, his colour, and the grey developing around his mouth which were the signs of his older age. Whilst I told my audience all of this, I had his bag of treats next to me which I then showed to the audience. This was my way to get Indigo's attention to come and sit next to me in the chair.

Apologising to my audience, I explained my screen would wobble whilst I moved it to show Indigo. It worked really well. It gave the audience a sense of the character I was talking about. Indigo happily chomped on the biscuit I had in my hand whilst I held the laptop steady in front of his face, showing him off.

My Zoom talks became so popular that I ended up doing almost one a week. As I became more experienced delivering talks in this way, I began to hone the process. I became adept at making sure there was enough lighting in front of my face and set up my phone to give me subtitles when questions were asked. Indigo's uniform was ready to show, in addition to the cooker timer I used. Ralph used to say that I had turned our dining room into a mini studio, such was the preparation I would carry out before a talk.

I enjoyed seeing the audiences and would chuckle to myself. I could see little brownies, girl guides and scouts bouncing around on the screen at home full of energy. Sometimes, they would be sitting still, listening earnestly and occasionally there would be a child picking their nose on the screen, forgetting they could be seen by everyone else on the call.

It was often touching when they would want to introduce me to their own dogs with usually mum or dad in the background supervising. Many of the dogs appeared to be happy to be accosted and plonked in front of their screen to be shown. Some of the questions the children asked were so thoughtful. One little girl asked me 'How did you manage before you had Indigo?' I admitted it had been hard, and that he was like the final piece of jigsaw in my life with regards to my deafness.

The talks were a fabulous way to stay connected with people in what was a difficult couple of years, with socialising seriously curtailed. The Hearing Dogs Community Fundraising Manager, Gaynor Cavanagh, would regularly thank me. She was appreciative of the money I was raising for the Charity by doing the talks and would often tell me I was 'a star.' It was a happy coincidence that she was also called Gaynor and our emails would often start with Hello Gaynor T and sign off as Gaynor C, and vice versa.

Sharing the joy of having Indigo with a much wider audience, up and down the country, was my happy place. I was therefore surprised in April 2021 when Gaynor texted me one day and asked me to read a recent blog on the Charity's website. As I logged on, I was gobsmacked. There, for all to see, was a testimony of my work as a volunteer for the Charity. I had been named April's volunteer of the month. It was an emotional moment. I realised just how much I had touched the lives of so many people, both within and outside of the Charity. It was down to being matched with Indigo, sharing with others about my life with him, that had made this all possible.

Retirement Beckons

Indigo was coming up to retirement. The Charity retires Labrador Retriever dogs at eleven years old. The smaller dogs retire a year or so later. The day was fast approaching, and I had been in long discussions with Andy, my partnership instructor. We had started the application process to find Indigo's successor a year previously. It was not something I was relishing. Indigo had been my ears for the past 9 years and we had an incredible bond. My main focus was that Indigo would still enjoy a happy retirement in our home, as a pet.

The Charity offers a number of options when a hearing dog retires. The first option available is to wait until their death before you apply for another hearing dog. Another option is to apply for a successor dog and when a suitable match is found, the Charity take the retired hearing dog and find an alternative, suitable home. This option is open for those who may live on their own and work full-time, not enabling them to care both for their new hearing dog and the retired dog.

The next option is for the retired hearing dog to be given to a friend of the recipient when their successor dog arrives. I had opted for the final option. Indigo was to remain with us as the family pet. I wanted to ensure that Indigo remained happy with a new successor dog in our home. It is fortunate that Ralph was able to stay at home, and I feel incredibly lucky to have this option. We had decided that Indigo would become his walking companion when I am out at work for two and half days a week.

I had noticed that Indigo was slowing down. He was still able to alert me to sounds, but I noticed at work he was less keen to keep moving between the various offices. He would often appear more tired in an evening. It was important to me, first and foremost, that a new dog was able to play nicely with Indigo and for them both to get along. Indigo was happy. I wanted him to be comfortable in his home, in his old age. I explained all of this to Andy, and as Easter 2021 approached for Indigo's retirement, it was with some sadness when I posted his uniform back to the Charity. I reflected that Indigo had been the most amazing hearing dog. A new dog had huge paws to fill.

The Challenge of Great Gable

Indigo's retirement was a big milestone. I too started to think about setting my own new challenges, before Indigo became too old and unable to join me. Moving to the Lakes, we were surrounded by the most stunning mountain scenery; it was one of our decisions to move to this area, for the beauty and magnificence of the mountains. One of our canoe trips was Wasdale with the majesty of Great Gable looming before us at the head of the lake.

The summit of the mountain seemed tantalisingly within reach, and yet, at 899 metres, I knew it was a huge undertaking of a walk. Not something to take lightly. In addition, walking an older dog to these heights, was a responsibility. Indigo happily came out with me on my runs twice a week. However, I was aware that mountain walking presented a different set of challenges. The distance and the terrain needed to be considered. My questions were as such: would Indigo be able to tackle a walk of at least five hours? Would he be fit enough? Would there be enough water for him to drink?

In preparation, Ralph did a trial walk on his own, finding the most suitable route to the summit that would not involve hanging off a cliff. Moreover, we needed plenty of freshwater streams for Indigo to access to ensure he kept cool and hydrated. Having identified the best route, we set out to climb the mountain on a clear sunny day in April. Our rucksacks were packed with water, food, waterproofs, and extra layers. It was a glorious start with Indigo clearly enjoying different smells and sights. I had not climbed a mountain of this magnitude for a year or so but had completed Black Combe at 600 metres a few weeks previously, getting my legs accustomed to going up hills again.

We gained height and the route chosen turned out to be perfect for both me and Indigo. I am not keen on scree or rock climbing, and we are always conscious of Indigo's safety when on the Fells. This was a relatively gentle climb. As we neared the final path to the summit, I sat on the grass with Indigo absorbing the stunning visas and views and warily looked up at the last pathway to the top.

I took a deep breath; I was determined to reach the top and clearly Indigo felt the same. We finally reached the summit and as I sat eating my sandwich, I considered the remarkable achievement that Indigo had accomplished. It felt such a fitting way to mark his retirement whilst still fit enough to do so. We still had the long return walk ahead of us. However, it was now downhill all the way, and it was just a case of taking our time and pause to enjoy the stunning views. It was with some relief when we were back in the car park. My legs complained about the unfamiliar exertion that they had been put through. It was not only Indigo who slept well that night.

New Kid on the Block

It was a huge change for me not having a canine partner by my side. Shopping whilst wearing masks was confusing and difficult. I struggled to understand the world around me. I started to avoid going into shops as much as I could. It was no longer obvious that I was deaf and I found it difficult to explain that I relied on lipreading without Indigo by my side. I noticed that people around me were also anxious such was the effect of this unknown virus.

In May, to my surprise, I received the email I had been hoping for. The Charity informed me that a match may have been found; was I interested? I don't think I could have replied any quicker. The answer was a resounding yes. Photos followed promptly of the most gorgeous small female black Labrador named Velma.

In order to settle Velma into her new home, I made arrangements to take some annual leave. During COVID, the placement was very different to the one I had experienced in 2012. No stay overnight at the Centre to meet Velma. This time, I was to see her via a Microsoft Teams meeting through my laptop. There, on the screen, I could see this beautiful Labrador bitch, curled up contentedly, next to the trainer, Matt.

We discussed how Velma was going to be placed with me. In her first few weeks, she would be a companion pet dog, settling into her new environment. Discussions involved how we would introduce her to Indigo. We agreed that when Matt arrived with Velma, we would take both dogs for a walk on neutral territory, in order for them to become accustomed to each other.

June 1st 2021 arrived. I eagerly waited for the pup van to arrive. I looked at Indigo and told him that his life was going to change irrevocably with this new arrival. He looked up at me, enjoying the extra attention and cuddles he was receiving and of course not knowing that from this moment on, his life would never be quite the same again.

The pup van arrived and was a glorious sight. Emblazoned with photos of Hearing Dogs across its paintwork and the Charity's distinctive logo. Matt and I agreed that Velma would want to stretch her legs and so would meet Indigo on our front lawn. We planned to take them immediately after, for a walk together. It proved to be an excellent way to introduce them. The van door opened and out leaped this energetic ball of fur whizzing around on the front lawn. It was with pleasure that I noted Indigo happily trotting behind Velma, enjoying a new playmate completely nonplussed at watching this burst of bouncy Labrador.

Setting off for the walk, Matt and fell into an easy chat. Velma happily sniffed her way along her new territory and Indigo followed behind, knowing his familiar route well. As we took them to the beach, I had been forewarned that Velma loved playing with a ball. I had often thrown a ball for Indigo but usually he was just happy to be on the beach, rolling in the sand, enjoying the fine grit on his back. However, if another dog ran for a ball, he happily joined the chase. It was with pleasure, I noted that this happened with Velma and her ball.

During the walk back to our bungalow, Matt gave me a heads up on what to expect overnight with Velma. I was told not to worry if she was up a few times in the night or was heard making distressed noises. He had booked into a local B&B and assured me he was contactable by text should I need him. As he left, Velma decided she would have a play with Indigo, and the two of them rolled around in the garden, giving off delightful noises with both their mouths open.

This familiar dog behaviour is called mouthing or jaw sparring. A healthy way for a dog to play with other dogs. I was aware that mouthing mimics an actual fight, but without the serious biting. It was a delight to observe, it meant that both Indigo and Velma were already very relaxed in each other's company. I filmed their play on my phone and immediately sent it to Matt, showing their playful nature together. Matt replied that it looked so sweet, and he was 'So happy.'

The first overnight with Velma went well. She needed her customary toilet in the middle of the night and settled in her bed. Ralph told me that no distress noises were to be heard. The next morning, Matt arrived checking on how our first night had gone. Walking into the garden, he was greeted by Velma as she gave him a happy wag of her tail. She then sauntered back into the garden as if to say: 'Nice to see you but this is my home now.' At that moment, I felt a bit sorry for Matt. He had been her trainer for the last six months and I could not imagine how it must have felt. However, it did feel as though Velma instinctively knew; this was going to be her new permanent home.

Big Paws to Fill

Indigo was incredibly patient with Velma whilst she settled into a new routine and home. She tried to pinch his food after she had gobbled all of hers. I took the time to work with her on this. Making her wait and stay, whilst Indigo's food would be put down first. It worked well and by the time she had polished off her food, Indigo had eaten all his.

The two of them get on so well and have great fun playing together, sharing toys without any hint of jealousy from either of them. My main concern was always to ensure that Indigo was happy and content. He clearly was, it was a huge relief for me. We started to introduce the sound work to her and it was interesting to observe Indigo's behaviour. If Velma was a bit hesitant in her response when hearing the sounds, Indigo would appear, nudge me, look at Velma as if to say: 'C'mon, this is what we do.'

Velma quickly became more familiar to her new home environment and confident in responding to the sound work. Indigo sensed this, started to stand back, and let her do the work, knowing he would still get his treats. I noted his gentle slide into retirement. The two weeks of my annual leave flew past, and as Indigo showed his gentle spirit, he also displayed a new lease of life. Acting more and more like a puppy again, rolling around on the floor with Velma. He clearly enjoyed his play tugging with the toys, together. It was everything I had hoped for, a happy fun-filled life for Indigo in his twilight years.

I continued to send videos of our sound work to the trainer. Updating him on Velma's progress, she demonstrated excellent alerts to all the sounds around the house. It was therefore no surprise that she gained the right to proudly wear her uniform in record time; within just three weeks of her arrival.

The day approached when it was time to take Velma to work at the prison with me, for the first time. As I stood in front of the imposing steel gates looming high above me, I thought about how I had felt the first time with Indigo, only a few years previously. As Velma gazed up at me, her soft warm brown eyes seemed to say: 'What are we doing mum?' I took a deep breath. Looked down at her and said: 'We've got this buddy.

Photos

Baby photo

Nursery school - a rather ironic photo with a telephone!

From Left to right

London Marathon – running for Hearing Dogs for Deaf People

Graduation for Community Justice degree – spot Sheila Hancock as honory guest!

HMP Haverigg

From top to bottom -Cone head Indigo

Photoshoot at BWC

Jo and Paul, Indigo's Bed and Breakfast volunteers - meet Indigo again.

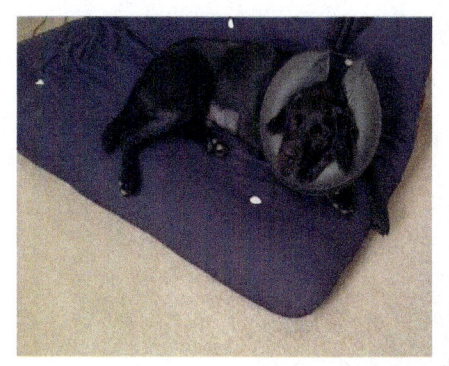

From top to bottom

Indigo meets Cocoa at Ilfracombe Chocolate Emporium

Sandy faced boy!

Canoeing the Lakes

Crufts and the Hearing Dogs for Deaf stand in 2019

Indigo meets sister, Inca at Crufts in 2019

From top to bottom - Selfie with Indigo
- Indigo enjoying his retirement and walks with Ralph
- Conquering Great Gable just before Indigo retired 2021

From top to bottom
- Indigo and Velma enjoying a game
- Indigo and Velma enjoying their snuggles

From top to bottom
- Volunteering for the wonderful charity with Indigo
- Volunteer of the month from Hearing Dogs April 2021
- Great British dog walk for Hearing Dogs - One of the many fundraisings events Indigo and I attend – photo courtesy of Ami 'Mim' Botly.

From top to bottom
- Selfie with Indigo and Velma
- Indigo around Millom

Printed in Great Britain
by Amazon